corporate
agility

INSIGHTS ON **AGILE PRACTICES** FOR
ADAPTIVE, COLLABORATIVE, RAPID,
AND TRANSPARENT ENTERPRISES

MICHAEL WONG

corporate agility

INSIGHTS ON **AGILE PRACTICES** FOR ADAPTIVE, COLLABORATIVE, RAPID, AND TRANSPARENT ENTERPRISES

WILEY

Agilessons™ is a trademark of DayBlink.

Published by John Wiley & Sons, Inc., Hoboken, New Jersey.

Published simultaneously in Canada.

Photography by Michael Will, Matthew D. Hodges, John Andrada-www.jandradaphotography.com, and professional headshots provided by each contributor.

For general information on our other products and services or for technical support, please contact our Customer Care Department within the United States at (800) 762-2974, outside the United States at (317) 572-3993 or fax (317) 572-4002.

Wiley publishes in a variety of print and electronic formats and by print-on-demand. Some material included with standard print versions of this book may not be included in e-books or in print-on-demand. If this book refers to media such as a CD or DVD that is not included in the version you purchased, you may download this material at http://booksupport.wiley.com. For more information about Wiley products, visit www.wiley.com.

Library of Congress Cataloging-in-Publication Data is Available:

ISBN 9781119652267 (Paperback)

ISBN 9781119652281 (ePDF)

ISBN 9781119652212 (ePub)

Cover Design: Wiley

Cover Image: © D_A_S_H_U/Getty Images

Printed in the United States of America

SKY10020448_081420

To all the genuinely people-centric corporations that endeavor to uplift the human experience while delivering on the opportunities of capitalism.

To my parents, Ron and Tesi, who successfully navigated our family through the challenges and joys of middle-class America.

And to my Sorin, Melina, Lennon, and Maryn, thank you for your love, support, and sacrifices while Daddy focused on this project.

CONTENTS

INTRODUCTION

Aloha! When Wiley first approached me to collaborate on a book, I was a bit apprehensive. The time required to research, plan, and write a thoughtful and novel book would be challenging, to say the least. It wasn't until we landed on a subject that was both timely and broadly applicable to my corporate clients that I agreed to join them on this challenging and rewarding journey. From my time growing up in Hawai'i to founding my own company, DayBlink Consulting, I've experienced my fair share of ups and downs. Through them all, I've learned and lived a core value

DayBlink Team, February 7, 2020

which was taught to me at a young age – keep people at the forefront, whether it's family, team members, or customers. That's why, when I first came across Agile, I knew it was a special way of working and one I needed to champion, to help others understand the ideas that gave so much to me.

If you've picked up this book, you're most likely already familiar with how Agile frameworks, toolkits, and practices have transformed parts of the business world. What was once just an approach to software development, Agile has become an increasingly viable and present methodology employed by some of the largest, most successful corporations and organizations worldwide, including Microsoft, AT&T, Google, Spotify, IBM, 3M, and more.[1,2] In fact, even the United States federal government requires an Agile methodology be used for many of their IT contracts and in some other non-IT sectors as well.[3] Whether you want to increase revenue, innovate technology, engage your workforce, or be able to thrive under uncertainty and rapid change, Agile approaches all challenges head on with one common theme: to get things done rapidly. Whatever your aim may be, corporate agility may be a prudent path to pursue.

Still, many leaders will fail to see its potential. According to a global survey by CA Technologies, despite increased awareness of Agile methods at the corporate level, executives still acknowledge them primarily as solutions related to software development and IT.[4] This sentiment is due in part to a misunderstanding or misrepresentation of Agile: to many, it is an overused word that comes with its share of baggage. Despite this notion, I'm sure at some point, someone has tried to sell you Agile, pushing something that sounded too good to be true. Though passionate and with good intention, some of these Agile zealots undermine what being agile has to offer. They preach the processes and frameworks which, without a true understanding of the timeless truths embedded in the values and principles of the Agile Manifesto, will result in just doing Agile for the sake of Agile.

For those truly wanting to learn, *'ike loa*, and pursue corporate agility, this book seeks to dispel the aforementioned confusion about Agile. When utilized with forethought, deliberation, and careful consideration, Agile can be used to successfully navigate through the constant disruptions and changes that corporations face. For over twenty years, I've worked as a strategic management consultant advising hundreds of companies to develop their strategies, implement new programs, and deliver market value. In this time I've found that what clients really want, what humans inherently seek, is clarity and results. I don't want to just demystify Agile – I want people to understand and internalize these timeless truths, in a pragmatic way, so they can use them to realize their goals. With the lessons in this book, you'll explore how Agile can be applied within and across the corporation to achieve your goals and desired results.

To demystify Agile, first understand its origins. Ideas similar to the values and principles of Agile first appeared in the 1970s. In the 1990s, startups and smaller organizations began utilizing these ideas, helping them execute faster than top-down, hierarchical models ever did. It wasn't until the new millennium, however, that a group of seventeen software developers, holed up in a snowy resort in Utah, came to define Agile in a more comprehensive, unified way. As a group, they published the Manifesto for Agile Software Development, popularly known as the Agile Manifesto.

Following the creation of the Agile Manifesto, Agile began proliferating in the larger corporations that had shied away from it before. And while some have found success, many others have discovered that Agile is just not that easy. This is because Agile is often approached as a one-size-fits-all solution. However, it's quite the opposite. A startup's Agile journey will be vastly different from that of a global corporation. It is important to understand these differences and account for the various styles of management, work cultures, and what is considered business as usual. This doesn't mean, however, that one has a better chance of success than the other; it just means that the path to corporate agility will be different, and that's okay! Agile can be flexible when used correctly. It's all about understanding how best it can be applied in your corporation.

Do not be swayed by particular Agile success stories or tales of failures. Instead, look to agilists who have had multiple experiences of transforming corporations and can help you understand, objectively, what separated corporations that succeeded from corporations that failed. Luckily, you're reading this book. It utilizes a data-driven approach, compiling case studies, first-hand interviews, professional experiences, and actionable advice to help get you started on your unique path to corporate agility. And while there are already many tactical "how-to" books on Agile, I've decided instead to focus on what the data suggests, and highlight why, therefore, and how, strategically – an objective perspective on both the good and bad of Agile that will be shared with you.

Ultimately, your enterprise's success or failure depends on the people within. I truly believe this and actually founded DayBlink on this principle: our greatest asset is our people, our family, our *'ohana*, and that to be excellent, we have to keep this mentality at the forefront. Through this approach we have achieved incredible growth and obtained numerous awards since our inception, like 2018's Fastest Growing Firms as awarded by *Consulting* magazine. And we practice what we preach – we are an Agile-driven company.

Formed with our people first, it's not hard to see why our values and principles, like trust and continuous improvement, are so similar with that of Agile. So much so, that the DayBlink journey, our *huaka'i pilikin*, from an older way of working to Agile, was seamless. Over the years, Agile has further proliferated and expanded within DayBlink, its values eventually driving all of our actions. In fact, this very book was developed and written utilizing incremental releases and continuous feedback from readers like you.

On a parting note, I want to clarify that I am not pushing a particular agenda. In fact, quite the opposite. I'm always the first to say that Agile is not the answer for everyone. It's a long and arduous journey to get it right. But when you do, well, you'll just have to read on to find out.

Michael Wong
Founder, DayBlink
2020

Distinguished Contributors

DISTINGUISHED CONTRIBUTORS

Arie van Bennekum
Agile Manifesto, Co-Author
Wemanity Group, Thoughtleader
Arie has a background as a developer and technical designer, with over 30 years experience in Agile transformations. He believes people are the component that makes Agile successful.

Marcus Johnson
Highmark Health, SVP, Enterprise Effectiveness
Marcus is a seasoned executive helping companies realize financial and operational excellence through large scale business transformation. He brings consulting and industry experience to lead change in areas including: operating model design, process optimization, automation, and Agile.

Louis Toth
Comcast Ventures, Co-Founder
Louis is a co-founder and former managing partner at Comcast Ventures, helping Comcast innovate for over 20 years. He has prior experience in Investment Banking and holds both undergraduate and graduate degrees from the University of Pennsylvania.

Phil Koserowski
The Leading Hotels of the World, VP, Marketing Executive
As VP at The Leading Hotels of the World, Phil is responsible for LHW's Global brand strategy, customer acquisition, engagement and loyalty as well as customer facing touchpoints including web, mobile, advertising, social media and emerging channels.

Allen Broome
MediaKind, CTO
Allen is an experienced technology executive with expertise in consulting, software engineering, and successful product development utilizing Agile methodologies.

Vamsi Tirnati
DXC Technology, CTO of Transportation
Vamsi is an accomplished Global Enterprise IT leader with over 22 years of experience defining and executing technology strategy and digital transformations with innovative and growth-oriented solutions for F100 companies.

Michael Piker
Philip Morris International, VP, Global Total Rewards, Employee Relations, Agile Performance
Michael is a seasoned executive who is responsible for leading the transformation of Total Rewards, Employee Relations and Agile Performance Strategy at Philip Morris International (PMI) as they design a smoke-free future.

Steve Elliott
Atlassian, Head of Jira Align
Steve is an established software executive with 20 years of technology experience in a variety of industries. He is currently head of Jira Align at Atlassian, after his Agile company was acquired in 2019.

Max Ekesi
Whole Foods Market, Agile Program Manager
Max has over 12 years of experience leading IT Transformation efforts by leveraging Agile methodologies and building high functioning teams and cultures.

Kishore Koduri
Ameren, Director, Enterprise Architecture, Resilience and Agile Office
Kishore is an accomplished, competent, and goal-oriented thought leader in the Agile space with valuable experience transforming service and product-based organizations through the effective roll-out of Agile and user-centered culture.

Laurie Nicoletti
Mastercard, VP of Product Development
Laurie, a highly skilled and accomplished Agile Transformation Leader, focuses on product development, commanding PI planning sessions and WSJF backlog grooming with global teams.

Sondra Ashmore, Ph.D
Berkley Technology Services LLC, AVP and Business Partner
Sondra is the co-author of *Introduction to Agile Methods*. She has taught Agile to university students and has worked with Agile teams for over 12 years. She advises W.R. Berkley companies on leveraging technology to optimize business performance.

DISTINGUISHED CONTRIBUTORS

Gilli Aliotti
CBS Interactive, VP, Project Management
Gilli is an accomplished Senior Executive and thought leader with more than 25 years of success across the media, entertainment, information technology, education, nonprofit, and event management industries.

Anthony Olsen
Windstream Enterprise, Product Owner
Anthony specializes in mobile and web-based applications. His primary focus is managing CRM integrations and softphone launches using Agile methodologies.

Elaine Stone
Capital One, Director, Agile Portfolio, Consumer Identity
Elaine, a key leader in supporting Capital One's disruption of the financial services space, is a focused professional with wide-ranging experience in operations, Agile methodologies, process optimization, program and project management, and product management and strategy.

Dr. Steve Mayner
Scaled Agile, Inc., SAFe Fellow & Principal Consultant
Steve is an expert thought leader, speaker, coach, and consultant with over 30 years of proven performance successfully delivering customer-driven technology solutions and innovations.

Ashley Craft Fiore
Honeywell, Director, Agile Program Management
Ashley is a future-focused Technology Executive with substantial success directing digital transformation and software development strategies. She integrates her programming and architecture experience to help guide businesses while driving technological innovations.

Junius Rowland
AutoZone, IT Manager, Agile Delivery Office
Junius is an enthusiastic professional with substantiated successes in Enterprise Agile transformation, Information Systems, and Project Management. He has a passion for exceeding organizational goals by increasing productivity, improving quality, and reducing cost.

Joshua Jones
StrategyWise, CEO
A lifelong founder, Joshua leads StrategyWise, a leading data science consulting firm that helps clients maximize operational effectiveness through data science and artificial intelligence.

Susan Marricone
Honeywell, Director, Agility Transformation Leader
Susan Marricone is a transformation leader with experience in Business Agility and Agile. She energizes strategic alignment and operational excellence in enterprises of all sizes to set them up for success.

Scott Ambler
Disciplined Agile, Co-Founder
Project Management Institute (PMI), VP
Scott is the co-founder of Disciplined Agile (DA)–(acquired by PMI) and creator of the world's only comprehensive Agile body of knowledge that provides straightforward and practical guidance to help individuals, teams, and enterprises choose their "ways of working."

Michael K Sahota
SHIFT314, Speaker, Trainer, & Consultant
Michael has written two books and has received accolades on his Certified Agile Leadership Trainings. He guides and teaches leaders how to develop Evolutionary Capabilities through culture, leadership, and conscious change.

Steven HK Ma
No Moss Consulting, Chief Purpose Officer
Steven is an expert in Agile organizational design who inspires purpose-driven people at enterprise scale. His professional purpose is to make work more human from helping executives change mindsets; to coaching high-performing teams; to creating market-topping products.

Jennifer Morelli
Grant Thornton, Principal, Business Change Enablement
Jennifer specializes in large-scale business transformation relating to technology, organizational, and business process change. She has experience in the strategy, development, and delivery of organizational change management, communications, and training programs.

DISTINGUISHED CONTRIBUTORS

Linda Rising
Independent Consultant
Linda has authored or edited five books and numerous articles. She is an internationally known presenter on topics related to patterns, retrospectives, influence strategies, Agile development, and the change process. Further, Linda drives successful organizational change.

Stacey Ackerman
Agilify Coaching & Training, Founder
Stacey is an Agile trainer, coach, and marketing professional. She also writes on Agile marketing for MarTech Today and the Business Agility Institute. She is passionate about helping marketing organizations around the world learn how Agile Marketing can help them cut through the red tape and rapidly deliver high-quality campaigns.

Bob Payne
LitheSpeed, SVP, Agile Transformation
An early adopter of Extreme Programming (XP), Bob has worked exclusively as an Agile Coach and practitioner since 1999. Bob has engaged in Enterprise Agile Consulting with LitheSpeed as SVP of Agile Transformation.

David Fisher
North Highland, Principal
David is the global Agile change management lead at North Highland. He uses his knowledge and experience to accelerate mission-critical changes for clients and the community by coaching leaders and leading teams through transformational change.

Dave Witkin
Packaged Agile, Principal
A seasoned agilist focusing on large-scale transformation, Dave helps government agencies and their contractors realize the promise of Agile, reducing failure rates on large government software programs through training and coaching.

Art Moore
Clear Systems LLC, President
Art is a Lean-Agile coach, mentor, and trainer focused on helping individuals, teams, and organizations achieve corporate agility at sustainably higher levels. He has over thirty years of consulting and leadership experience in government and commercial sectors.

Crawfurd Hill
Encompass Corporation, Corporate Agility Director
Crawfurd has led Agile transformations across a wide variety of industries, with a foundation in digital development. He has a great ability to communicate and inspire change.

Colin Ferguson
North Highland, Agile Transformation Principal
Colin has over 18 years of hands-on enterprise and team transformation experiences across many industries. He is known for his ability to coach and mentor team members and leadership to develop and embrace an Agile mindset.

Christen McLemore
HeyMac Consulting LLC, Founder
Christen has decades of practical experience coaching, leading Agile transformations and consulting Fortune 100 companies. Drawing from these experiences, she founded her own Agile consulting business, HeyMac Consulting, to make a greater impact focusing on the role of leaders and managers in Business Agility.

Joseph Murray, Ph.D
DayBlink Consulting, Partner
Joseph is a seasoned management consultant with extensive experience in the telecommunications and media sectors. Prior to joining DayBlink Consulting, he led and delivered numerous large-scale business transformations at companies across the globe while with Ericsson Consulting, KPMG, Deloitte Consulting, and AT&T.

corporate agility

INSIGHTS ON **AGILE PRACTICES** FOR ADAPTIVE, COLLABORATIVE, RAPID, AND TRANSPARENT ENTERPRISES

PART ONE

The Case for Corporate Agility

The need for adaptive and rapid evolution has never been greater. The time to change is now. Master the timeless "truths" of Agile and find your unique path to corporate agility.

CHAPTER 1

The Timeless Executive Challenge

In an era of accelerating change, executives deal with disruption on a regular basis. History teaches us that disruption is neither new nor is it going away. Embrace the opportunity that comes with disruption and transform your corporation into the organization of tomorrow.

Walter's world was upside down. There was a sense of normalcy as he departed Los Angeles, California. It was a critical business trip, maybe career defining, and Walter knew it. One of those make-or-break meetings awaited him in New York City. But the trip felt immeasurably longer than usual. Not in hours, not in distance, but in thoughts that were racing through his head. As he sat in his first-class seat, the cabin shook left and right, and up and down as he flew high above the Rocky Mountains. He grabbed his armrest and wondered how he was going to navigate his way out of this one. This seemed different.

Even though many of his friends and colleagues thought of him as a little too high-energy, Walter was well-liked and a capable, confident, charismatic, and driven leader.[1] Thinking back to his fast-tracked career, he realized he had a unique journey and experienced much in a short time. Far earlier than many of his contemporaries, he became CEO of the Midwest-based Laugh-O-Gram Corporation but, for various reasons, the corporation failed just two years after he took over the helm.[2] The industry was undergoing swift change and he placed a bet, putting his company ahead of anticipated customer demand. When the customers didn't materialize, neither did the revenue. Any executive in charge of a company that crashes and burns through the United States bankruptcy courts will have their confidence shaken.

But not Walter; he learned from this failure and pivoted. Even with the weight of significant financial hardship on his shoulders, he soldiered on, moved to Southern California, worked hard, and took his career in a completely different direction. Unfortunately, that failed, too. The move was too far outside his core strengths. He learned the lesson of being purposeful and intentional. Again, he took inventory, adjusted, and plotted his next move.[3]

Shortly thereafter, he returned to the C-suite of another company, Hyperion, where his long hours and innovative product vision would ultimately translate to significant financial success. Unfortunately, soon after the corporation's widely successful new product started churning cash, another business setback befell Walter.[4]

On his way out to New York City for his big meeting with Universal Studios, he received word. His worst fears were true. Everything he had worked so hard for at his latest company was gone. Due to a contractual loophole, Universal overtook the IP. To add insult to injury, he also found out that virtually all his talented developers whom he had hired and trained to support the product, and whom he had treated like family, had resigned and joined the newfound competitor. His team was gone, his trust in others shaken. He learned from this.[5]

This was another one of Walter's classic public failures. Instead of lawyering up and fighting for what one could argue was rightfully his, he returned to California. Though only days removed from an epic failure, Walter moved on. It was on his return trip home that he developed his next innovation and career defining accomplishment … Mortimer.

Failure wasn't going to deter this determined man. He was excited about this new direction. Pulling from the lessons he had learned in the past, he built a new team, modified his management style, and focused on Mortimer. But his wife, Lillian, wasn't convinced Mortimer was the right name; sounds a little too pompous for her liking.[6] Accepting feedback from anyone, including his inner circle, was unnatural for Walter, but he trusted Lillian, so he listened to her advice. There was no "team" member closer to him than his wife; there was unquestioning trust. Walter, or Walt as many of his friends and colleagues called him, decided to rename his new creative offering. Mortimer Mouse became Mickey Mouse, who grew to be the most popular animated character known around the world.[7]

The story of Walt Disney's struggles and successes are well-documented. Though nearly a century ago, the challenges that Walt faced still exist today. Characters and storyline details differ, but lessons about disruptors (failure, trust, team, and purpose) apply to executives in the Fortune 500 today just as they did a hundred years ago – and they will a hundred years hence. The challenges executives face today are not unique in history. The themes repeat themselves. They are timeless.

Stakes Are High

Data shows that Fortune 500 companies and their executives are experiencing greater volatility than ever before, a reality that will only continue to proliferate.

The obstacles that Walt faced and overcame on his path to success are neither unique to him nor his time; rather, they are situations that every executive will likely encounter on their own journey. Take, for example, today's leaders who must work to keep their organizations relevant in an age of accelerating change. This change is caused by different levers; however, their solutions stay the same, but more on that later.

For example, consider that companies in 1965 stayed in the S&P 500 index for an average of 33 years.[8] By 1990, that tenure had diminished to 20 years. Over the next few decades, the rate has continued to fall to where it is now, where over half of the current S&P 500 companies are predicted to keep their title for less than 10 years. No matter the industry or sector, this forcing function is reality and will only continue to proliferate. To make matters worse, with the advent of globalization and modernized technologies, barriers to entry have fallen, giving way to large numbers of market newcomers. The large, more established corporations are beginning to lose to small, nimble ones that are better prepared to solve today's challenges and maneuver through today's changing environment, further exacerbating the volatility that large organizations feel. PwC shares this sentiment: "[Consider] the scale and pace of change – today's forces of disruption can shake up an entire industry sector in less time than it takes most companies to update their IT systems."[9]

Furthermore, long-running executives, who are armed with the tools to succeed in traditional environments, but not today's disruptive ones, are often unprepared to face these newcomers. To explain, a study from Innosight found that executives have a "confidence gap" or a blind spot regarding novel competition. This is because these executives believe their competition will come from existing players. This is not the case as small and mid-tier companies are often the most effective disruptors, quicker to adapt and deploy emerging technologies and modern ways of working. Recently, the amount of these market disruptors has risen, with more and more executives feeling the pressure. Not all have been able to deliver and, as such, average tenure for C-suite executives has decreased across the board.

Executive Team Tenure

The average tenure of the C-suite continued its decline into 2019, putting increased pressure on executives to deliver tangible results rapidly.

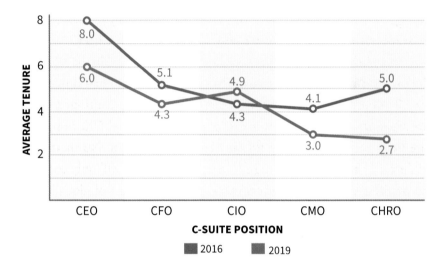

To make matters worse, the value an executive provides needs to match the salaries they receive. It's ultimately an ROI calculation. With corporations paying historically high salaries, executives must perform at their best from day one. Although this fact applies to all executive-level leaders, you can see this trend succinctly in the graph following, which showcases the rise of CEO salaries in the S&P 500 over the past 25 years. As this forcing function continues to proliferate, corporations will, likewise, continue to hold leaders accountable for more than just financial success. They will need to continually implement aspects relevant to today's day and age, like empowering employees, instilling a

The Age-Old Executive Challenge

Louis Toth
Comcast Ventures, Co-Founder

After a stint in Investment Banking and earning his MBA at Wharton, Louis Toth co-founded Comcast Ventures to help Comcast innovate for over twenty years. Through this experience, Toth found one thing to be clear: "When you have any large organization with hundreds of thousands of employees, trying to get that organization to think about the future is difficult." Toth stresses that those who are unable to circumvent this are likely to experience the same demise as once-behemoths like Blockbuster, Eastman Kodak, and others, especially in today's disruptive day and age.

Toth believes incentivization is an impediment to this shift from a short-term mindset, especially at the "leadership level, whose compensation is tied to quarterly results – it's hard for them to be thinking anything other than tactically." To illustrate, Toth cites the early stages of Coronavirus disease (COVID-19) Pandemic in the United States: "Many were watching and listening. They knew how severe it was in other parts of the world. Still, we couldn't see the immediate impact and behavior didn't change until it was too late."

Although this shift is paramount, Toth stresses that "the vast majority of people, frankly, will not be able to grasp it on their own." As such, he suggests leadership employ a pertinent tactic: "The first step is always to find those that are there for the long term, either because they're dedicated to making a career out of the company or they are truly passionate about the product. Whatever it is, find these agents within the organization and arm them with the right kind of ideas. Then, that mindset can proliferate to others."

Using this approach, Toth found much success with the various investments at Comcast Ventures for over two decades. Recently, he has transitioned his expertise to an advisor role at Touchdown Ventures and co-manages his own fund, Alter Venture Partners. Wherever he is, however, Toth always holds true to his original advice: "Thinking about the future is hard. Organizations that do are set up to succeed."

culture of trust, and adapting to the social responsibility landscape, among many others. Again, not all will be able to adjust to the increased responsibilities and to the changes of today.

S&P 500 Executive Compensation

Executive compensation continues to reach historical heights year after year; with higher compensation comes increased pressure and expectations.

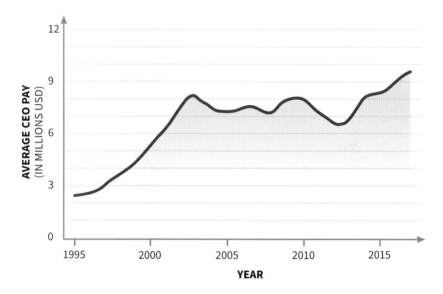

Source: Adapted from David Larcker and Brian Tayan, 2019[11]

The Future of Work

The workplace of tomorrow will continue to change as the technology used and the people within constantly evolve.

Modern technologies continue to evolve at an ever faster rate and in different directions. To compete, organizations must comprehend and confront these changes, as they inevitably become the status quo. This need is further necessitated as consumers are constantly demanding more efficient, digitized solutions. Remember, however, akin to the executive challenges described earlier, emerging technologies and changing customer preferences are not disruptions that are unique to today.

Take, for example, the development of computers and the World Wide Web in the 1960s. Prior to this, the workplace was vastly different: slides were hand-drawn, errors were covered with Tipp-Ex, and executive letters were dictated. Another example: the advent of the cellular network and smartphones just 20 years later, disrupting older, more traditional methods of communication. As emerging technologies continue to proliferate and expand, the forces of today – big data and analytics, blockchain, and automation, among many others – must be accounted for to not only compete, but thrive. PwC puts it succinctly: "Technology will continue to be both a source of disruption and an important way of turning disruption into opportunity."[12]

Big Data and Analytics

Big data has always been an instrumental tool that companies use to inform and drive business decisions. Many companies, however, fail to realize that data, combined with the advent of modern technologies and techniques, can provide much more value, in many different ways. Joshua Jones, CEO of StrategyWise, a leading AI and analytics firm, has experienced this first hand. He explains: "Firms often capture data for a specific purpose, but give no thought into how that data could be used elsewhere; these are lost opportunities."

Take, for example, a company that was able to get around this siloed mindset: Netflix. Its use of rating and genre data to build the "Cinematch" algorithm, the movie recommendation engine, enabled the company to grow from $5 million in revenues in 1999 to $8.3 billion in 2016.[13] It's important to note, however, that using big data and analytics was not Netflix's strategy; rather, it was a tool to augment and optimize capabilities to realize their strategy.

> "Firms often capture data for a specific purpose, but give no thought to how that data could be used elsewhere; these are lost opportunities."
>
> **Joshua Jones,** *StrategyWise*

Big data and analytics can be used in myriad beneficial ways by corporations. A relatively recent use case is within HR departments. Corporations have begun to use past employment data from prospective employees during the hiring process. Combined with advanced modeling and other statistical techniques, recruiters can now better predict the performance of potential hires, leading to more streamlined and effective hiring decisions.[14]

Another example: organizations are using process data to drive increased productivity within the corporation. Dan Enthoven, former CMO of Enkata, has been able to utilize this to optimize his client teams' day-to-day processes.[15] For example, he can analyze what separates the top and bottom performers: Do the best check emails less often? Do they read publications from better sources? Whatever they are, the data will help uncover it, enabling more efficient and productive workforces.[16]

Blockchain

Blockchain is one of those technologies that many people know about, but few understand. Most of their exposure to blockchain comes from its relationship with Bitcoin. Its use cases, however, have evolved past just commercial cryptocurrencies. Organizations are now using the technology to both bolster their privacy and security measures and reduce operating and transactional costs.

Take, for example, Walmart and its adoption of blockchain to prevent the spread of food-borne disease. The retail giant found that, after an outbreak, it could take days or even weeks to find the source. Better traceability would help Walmart take the appropriate actions rapidly and more effectively. To achieve this, they implemented blockchain technology and, through a proof of concept, were able to decrease the time needed to trace mangoes in the United States from 7 days to 2.2 seconds.[17] By applying this technology to other products, Walmart will be able to mitigate the severity of future outbreaks.

Blockchain will also disrupt functions that traditionally were immune to emerging technologies. One function in particular, Human Resources, is generally agreed upon as one of the most sound use cases within the enterprise. For example, with blockchain technology, organizations will be able to access immutable work history records, leverage smart contracts for contingent workers, and pay their employees directly. As blockchain technology becomes more mainstream and accessible, use cases will continue to expand into other parts of the enterprise. This phenomenon will be bolstered further by the continuous need for reliable, streamlined, and unambiguous data.

Automation

Automation will continue to disrupt the job market. Repetitious jobs, from customer representatives to truck drivers, are being replaced. In the future, however, jobs traditionally considered safe from automation – executives, middle managers, and others – will also be in danger. This phenomenon is better understood through a McKinsey & Company analysis, which found that 25% of a CEO's job can be handled by robots, and 35% of management tasks can be automated.[18] The following figure shows how disruptive automation will be to the job market, with 25% of jobs being affected in a high capacity due to the advent of these technologies. Another 36% of jobs will also be affected in a moderate capacity. This is the reality that enterprises need to understand and adjust to.

With that said, corporations should not dismiss those people whose jobs can be automated away; rather, they will find it more beneficial to retrain and repurpose these valuable employees. Joshua Jones provides strong insight here: "We're seeing firms everywhere begin to focus on providing data literacy training and tools to help the entire workforce stay relevant as technology changes. If you've got a 20,000 employee account in an industry that is clearly antiquated or moving away, you're going to have pain points if you don't make changes. Start by retraining people. Wherever possible, start putting people in other areas."

Impact of Automation

The increased adoption of automation is widely anticipated to displace more workers by 2025.

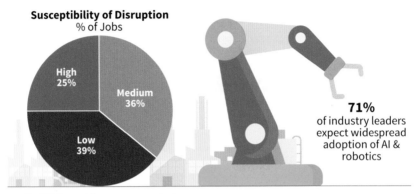

Susceptibility of Disruption
% of Jobs

High 25%
Medium 36%
Low 39%

71%
of industry leaders expect widespread adoption of AI & robotics

By **2025** machines are expected to perform more tasks that are currently done by humans

Source: Adapted from Amit Chowdhry, 2018; Valamis, 2018; David Greenfield, 2019[13]

This idea is further echoed by Bill Gates, co-founder of Microsoft, who said "displaced workers could fill gaps that currently exist elsewhere in the labor market – like elder care, teaching, and support for special needs children." And while Gates discussed roles outside of the corporation, the conversion within is apt. Organizations will continue to have gaps in certain functions like risk management and business continuity development among many others.[20, 21]

Besides the evolution of technology, that of the workforce will also continue. Although the values of today's younger generation represent a smaller piece of the pie, that portion will only continue to grow until those values become the workplace norm. As every new generation enters the workforce and the previous moves into retirement, the mix changes. Again, this change is not a unique phenomenon. In the past, corporations have had to adjust to the generational needs and wants of the workforce. They must continue to do so now, as they will need to in the future.

The Gig Economy

Just as new technologies are changing how work gets done, the job market is evolving as well, along with what is considered a "normal career." Long gone are the days of living for the gold watch after thirty years of service to a single company. On average, today's employees change jobs every five to seven years.[22] This is a fact; be prepared for this uncertainty.

Furthermore, these employees are increasingly choosing contingent work over a traditional career path. Whether it be to fit in with existing lifestyles, such as caring for children or aging parents, or simply because they prefer the freedom of independent work, many people today want a type of flexibility that was not possible, or was frowned upon, just twenty years ago. There may be less job security, as has been proven by the coronavirus disease (COVID-19) pandemic, but there is also higher pay in the short term, an attractive incentive for many. Organizations are beginning to leverage these workers by engaging them for meaningful short-term employment, especially when their teams need a helping hand or specialized knowledge for a certain project.

Generational Values

Generational values disrupt the workforce as the distribution of employees inherently changes over time. For example, in today's information age, Millennials and Gen Zers don't see clocking in and holding out for the aforementioned gold watch as fitting on their spectrum of career goals. Instead, they want a meaningful job, the ability to work with a purpose. To illustrate, a Deloitte study found that 76% of Millennials view businesses as a source of powerful social impact. As such, organizations with strong brand values and mission statements are often more popular with the new generation.[23]

Another generational value is the focus on a synergistic and innovative culture. Millennials and Gen Zers are increasingly prioritizing these environments, with many willing to switch companies to realize such

Spotlight

A Modern Look
at Digital Strategies

Joshua Jones
StrategyWise, CEO

Over the years, Joshua Jones has successfully founded numerous startups, across various industries including operations management, technology, healthcare, and marketing. His most recent venture, StrategyWise, a leading data science consulting firm, was ideated through the notion that "the shift toward digital experiences is a fast-moving trend that will only continue to proliferate." Jones and his team at StrategyWise help organizations leverage data analytics and artificial intelligence to adapt alongside this shift.

Jones has found through his engagements with Fortune 500 companies that the use of data is often an area where strategy is not prioritized enough. Corporations are quick to invest in the latest trends and technologies without truly understanding how they drive business value. He stresses, "In order to be able to truly leverage all the potential data can unlock, corporations should plan years in advance so they can be sure they are capturing and curating their data in a manner it can be used by their analytics teams."

Jones has found that data science and AI projects often fail due to the over-ambitious nature of their charter. Analytics teams often complain the largest two challenge areas are data quality and internal politics. Data quality concerns often arise when the project scope is too large, and too many sets of data are required – almost without fail some of those data will not be ready for use, and the project meets an untimely end. Similarly, internal politics often create a major roadblock by creating scope creep or otherwise creating too many variables or success factors for a single project to address.

To counter these challenges, Jones encourages his clients to employ an Agile thought process to each of their digital strategies – especially those in analytics and AI. He has found that "breaking down the strategy into smaller, more manageable chunks and implementing those chunks piece by piece, has helped many of these large organizations implement their digital strategies rapidly and effectively."

a culture. In fact, Fidelity Investments found that Millennials are willing to take a $7,600 pay cut to do so.[24] These values are just a few of many. Love it or hate it, they represent a portion of a pie that will increase over time until it becomes the status quo. When this happens, however, there will be another generation with values to account for, alluding to the original lesson: these challenges are not unique to today. They are timeless.

Reframing for the Future

Adapt and evolve to these rapid changes; those who do not may find themselves following in the footsteps of the once-greats: Blockbuster, RadioShack, Eastman Kodak, and Toys "R" Us.

To maneuver and find success in today's age of accelerating change, organizations must be willing to adapt and evolve. Max Ekesi, Agile Program Manager at Whole Foods Market, echoes this sentiment: "In order for us to succeed, and not just keep up the pace, but thrive, we have to be able to adapt at the speed of change, maybe even faster." Remember, however, that throughout history, corporations have faced the same challenges. How these challenges manifest has changed, but the levers to solve them have not, at least at a high level.

> "In order for us to succeed, and not just keep up the pace, but thrive, we have to be able to adapt at the speed of change, maybe even faster."
>
> **Max Ekesi,** *Whole Foods Market*

To meet these challenges, large-scale transformations are often necessary, completely overhauling mindsets and processes – a full transformation in how you, your colleagues, and teams work. Defined as a strategy, plan,

Spotlight

Adopting Agile in the Face of Disruption

Bob Payne
LitheSpeed, SVP, Agile Transformation

Bob Payne is a leading proponent of Agile methodologies and an early adopter of Extreme Programming (XP). Through his twenty-five years of experience training, coaching, and leading corporations toward corporate success and as an executive at leading change management organizations, Payne has gained a keen understanding of the benefits and outcomes a corporation can achieve as they progress along their transformation journey, Agile or otherwise, especially during volatile times of change.

To match these external disruptions, Payne believes it is important for corporations to begin disrupting from within. While these disruptions will initially be uncomfortable, Payne challenges leadership to understand potential benefits that can be derived from these shifts, including adaptiveness, flexibility, and innovation, among others. Payne adds that "[corporations] that understand the constant need to change will, over all time horizons, outperform others by a tremendous amount."

Payne adds that it is important for executives to understand that these transformations can often fail as they require the coordination and commitment from all involved. Payne goes on to caveat, however, that "what matters is taking that failure, learning from it, and applying those lessons moving forward." In inculcating this mindset, corporations will not shy away from failure; rather, they will embrace it as a learning opportunity on their path toward continued success.

Successfully implementing a transformation, Agile or otherwise, enables corporations to push the needle farther and farther, realizing capabilities and characteristics necessary to survive. Payne, however, coaches executives to understand that these journeys are continuous ones. "Make sure you are constantly self-evaluating and monitoring the change implemented." In doing so, corporations can move on from an older way of working to a more innovative and adaptive one in the future.

or process that gets you from where you are to where you need to be, a transformation is an apt and effective solution that corporations, regardless of when or where, have deployed to adapt to the challenges of their age.[25]

Those unable to transform fail to respond to disruption, and, in the end, collapse. Companies like RadioShack, Eastman Kodak, and Toys "R" Us all suffered this fate, as did Blockbuster. A crucial mistake by Blockbuster took place when Netflix approached the company and asked to be bought for $50 million. Blockbuster executives, unable to recognize the advent of changing customer preferences and of the digital distribution model, nearly laughed them out of the pitch room.[26] Lo and behold, a few years later, Blockbuster filed for bankruptcy. Blockbuster was an organization not open to change, to transforming themselves, and they paid for it.

Disruption of the Video Industry

Blockbuster's inability to react to disruptive threats led to their bankruptcy.

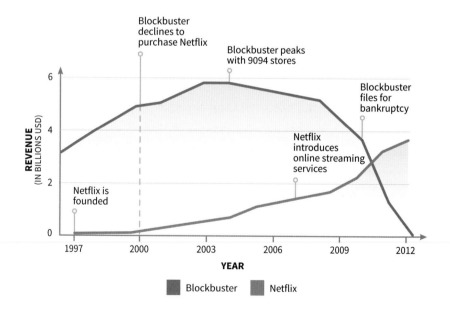

Source: Data from Jeanine Poggi, 2010; Ben Unglesbee, 2019; Brand Riddle, 2020. Adapted from Ramon Casadesus-Masanell and Karen Elterman, 2019[27]

On the other hand, an example of a successful transformation can be found in the journey of BlackBerry. In the early 2000s, BlackBerry was at the height of the telephone industry, akin to the Apple of today. However, over the course of the next few years, with the advent of market forces and disruptors combined with some poor business decisions, BlackBerry saw its stock drop over 80% and, at one point, considered a sale.[28] At the time when they were most vulnerable, BlackBerry adapted, pivoting toward cybersecurity. This move proved fruitful and allowed BlackBerry to reestablish as a market leader in a new industry.

Xerox's journey is another example of a successful transformation. In 2000, when ex-CEO Anne Mulcahy took the helm, the company was $18 billion in debt, toying with the idea of bankruptcy.[29] Although the business model was unsustainable, another change was necessary: the company culture. At one point, a customer even suggested: "You've got to kill the Xerox Culture [to survive]."[30] As such, Mulcahy championed Xerox and its values. Her company's employees responded, understanding what was at stake. The company would go on to pay off its debt and evolve its business model over the next eight years. "We wouldn't have survived if we didn't have that love and loyalty," Mulcahy would go on to say, highlighting how a transformed culture helped save the company.[31]

Although transformations will always be considered a primary method to adapt, the tools for implementing transformations have evolved. Over the past few decades, many organizations have used process improvement tools like Business Process Reengineering, Six Sigma, and Lean, among others, to transform. Others have used change management models like Kurt Lewin and Edgar Schein's "Three Stage Model" and Everett Rogers's "The Adoption Process." Recently, another approach has emerged and become increasingly popular with corporations as they strive to transform and achieve corporate agility. A unique way of thinking and working, Agile has proven valuable to organizations as they maneuver through today's challenging environment and transform themselves in the face of disruption.

CHAPTER 2

Decide if Agile Is Right for You

Be transparent about your purpose, strategic objectives, and desired operating model. Then, design your plan of action to realize them. All the while, consider the implications of adopting Agile and decide whether now is the time for you.

A Short Introduction to Agile

Recognize why Agile came about and how it has evolved.

A crisis emerged at the turn of the twenty-first century – businesses and their needs were moving far faster than their capabilities allowed, particularly in the context of software development. Termed "the development crisis," it described how enterprises would realize, partway through multi-year projects, that their needs and requirements had changed, negating most of the time and effort spent and decimating any progress made.[1]

Frustrated by this state of affairs, software thought leaders Jeff Sutherland, Arie van Bennekum, Alistair Cockburn, Jon Kern, and thirteen others began meeting and discussing ways to improve the process and circumvent the documentation overhead that led to the long development cycle times of traditional development approaches like waterfall.[2] They were already aware of this issue, having previously developed and implemented software development frameworks like Scrum, Crystal Clear, Extreme Programming (XP), and DSDM.

Determined to express and articulate a set of values and principles that underlay these frameworks and, more importantly, find ways of working that could overcome the development crisis, they held a special meeting in 2001, in the Wasatch Mountains of Utah. What emerged was the Agile Manifesto, which outlined four values and twelve principles that supported an overarching goal: to develop good products and get them to customers. Jeff Sutherland, one of the signatories and co-creator of Scrum, would go on to share a similar sentiment many years later: "Agile basically means iterating quickly, getting products in customers' hands."[3] This underlying theme of Agile and its manifesto underscores how beneficial being agile is as a way of thinking. The need to make and deliver good products is not a fundamentally new challenge; in fact it is quite the opposite – it is timeless.

Over the next two decades, the Agile Manifesto would fuel the evolution and adoption of the aforementioned frameworks and toolkits, and also pave the way for the advent of numerous others, including Scaled Agile Framework (SAFe), Disciplined Agile (DA), Large-Scale Scrum (LeSS), and Scrumban. There are few barriers to creating a new Agile framework or toolkit, except perhaps time. Since the Agile Manifesto is suggestive and not prescriptive, a new-fangled Agile framework can specify its own set of practices and terminology. That said, if the framework is to be taken seriously by many zealots in the Agile community, there is one constraint: these frameworks should be consistent with, and align to, the Agile values and principles, as would be evidenced by their specified ways of working.

The 2010s saw the rise of Agile frameworks and toolkits that could successfully scale across large corporations and deliver results. Cisco, for example, used SAFe to decrease the number of critical and major defects by 40% in their subscription billing platform, achieving the quality standards they had set out to reach.[4] Barclays, another example, used Disciplined Agile across more than 800 teams, and was able to increase throughput by 300% and support a monthly delivery frequency.[5]

But, Agile is not for everyone. Over the years since the publication of the Agile Manifesto, many companies jumped on the "Agile bandwagon" without proper consideration and preparation. As a result, many Agile transformations have failed, which in turn has led to negative misconceptions and stigmas. Furthermore, an Agile transformation will often come with an opportunity cost as you might defer or sacrifice other potential endeavors and initiatives. Whether forgoing a software refresh, M&A strategy, digitization implementation, or other such alternative initiatives, be mindful of what you're giving up when you choose to journey down the Agile path. As such, it's recommended that before you embark on such a journey, do your due diligence and consider the key steps discussed in the rest of this chapter.

Evolution of Agile

Over the years, many experts iterated on Agile themes, creating various frameworks and toolkits for a diverse array of contexts.

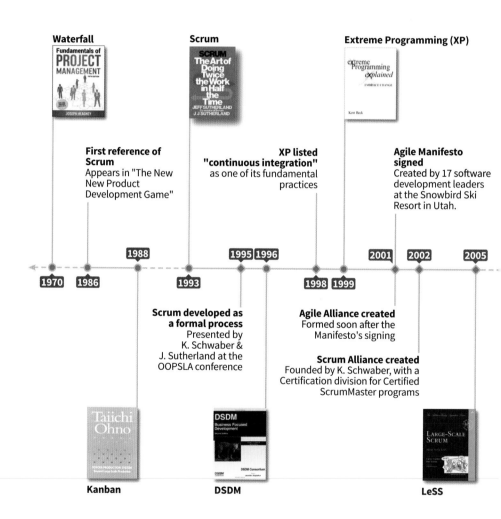

Waterfall

First reference of Scrum
Appears in "The New New Product Development Game"

Scrum

XP listed "continuous integration" as one of its fundamental practices

Extreme Programming (XP)

Agile Manifesto signed
Created by 17 software development leaders at the Snowbird Ski Resort in Utah.

1970   1986   1988   1993   1995   1996   1998   1999   2001   2002   2005

Scrum developed as a formal process
Presented by K. Schwaber & J. Sutherland at the OOPSLA conference

Agile Alliance created
Formed soon after the Manifesto's signing

Scrum Alliance created
Founded by K. Schwaber, with a Certification division for Certified ScrumMaster programs

Kanban

DSDM

LeSS

Source: Adapted from Jason Westland, 2018; Kendis Team, 2018; Agile Alliance, 2019; Robinson Meyer, 2015⁰

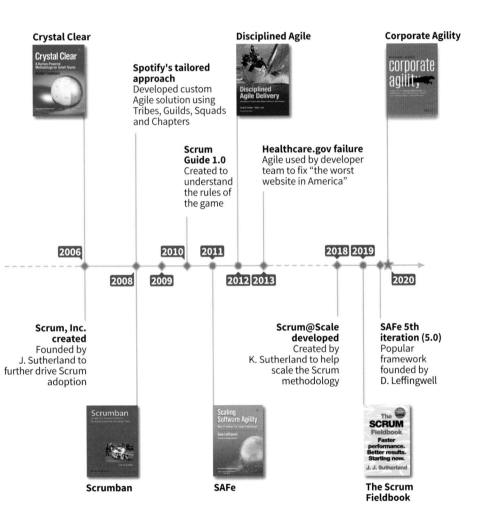

Crystal Clear

Spotify's tailored approach
Developed custom Agile solution using Tribes, Guilds, Squads and Chapters

Disciplined Agile

Corporate Agility

Scrum Guide 1.0
Created to understand the rules of the game

Healthcare.gov failure
Agile used by developer team to fix "the worst website in America"

2006
2008
2009
2010
2011
2012 2013
2018 2019
2020

Scrum, Inc. created
Founded by J. Sutherland to further drive Scrum adoption

Scrum@Scale developed
Created by K. Sutherland to help scale the Scrum methodology

SAFe 5th iteration (5.0)
Popular framework founded by D. Leffingwell

Scrumban

SAFe

The Scrum Fieldbook

Agile Bringing Change to Businesses

Arie van Bennekum
Agile Manifesto, Co-Author
Wemanity Group, Thought Leader

C o-Author of the Agile Manifesto, Arie van Bennekum has coached and guided numerous international Agile transformations across corporations and industries for the past twenty-plus years. He believes that although the original writing of Agile was grounded in software development practices, the underlying truths of Agile have always been applicable to all: "To be responsive to change and deliver the best value you can ... these are outcomes that every individual, team, and organization should strive for."

In line with this belief, van Bennekum has seen Agile proliferate out of software and IT departments, and into others like human resources and marketing. He believes that in today's world "Agile is becoming more and more a mainstream corporate capability no matter where in the organization you are." This fact is further becoming a reality as corporations begin to understand, to a certain extent, that they are only as good as their worst business unit, division, or department. By ingraining Agile across the business, all individuals, teams, and divisions can work together to collectively achieve the goals of a corporation.

Before transforming to Agile, however, van Bennekum warns his clients that this arduous journey will not be successful without leaderships' buy-in. He cites that "two years ago, the most important trend was corporate agility. The second was leadership. Any organization can embark on a journey, but without leaders championing at the front, the organization will not succeed."

Leadership buy-in is so important because "Agile requires a fundamental shift in habits and structures. Coaches are often looked to drive a transformation. And while they have the Agile background, how equipped are they to help people change behavior and mindsets? Not very well." Van Bennekum stresses that, to successfully transform to Agile, leaders of a corporation need to champion these shifts themselves and exhibit the change they want to see.

Know Your Corporation's Purpose

Determine what you are working toward before
engaging in any transformation.

Know your purpose. More specifically, know the answer to "Why does our corporation exist?" Though a bit existential, it's a critical place to start. In answering this question, you can more efficiently and clearly determine your enterprise's strategic objectives – faster time to market, reduced operating costs, differentiated products – and the desired operating model and characteristics within that are necessary to achieve those strategic objectives – flexible, responsive, efficient, collaborative. Once you understand what you are working toward, you can design and implement your plan of action.

This approach is akin to how a runner, depending on whether the runner wants to run a marathon or a 100m dash (the strategic objectives), will prioritize attaining endurance or explosiveness (the desired operating model and characteristics within) and achieve them through different types of training regimens (the plan of action to implement your operating model). "It's first about the organization and what the organization is trying to achieve, then you can get into the mindset of 'How can we achieve it?'" explained Gilli Aliotti, VP of Project Management at CBS Interactive.

> "It's first about the organization and what the organization is trying to achieve, then you can get into the mindset of 'How can we achieve it?'"
>
> **Gilli Aliotti**, *CBS Interactive*

Determining your strategic objectives and operating model isn't as easy as it seems; a first-year MBA would be quick to reply, "That's easy. Optimize shareholder value." Instead, it requires due diligence, experience, and effort. You will need to meet with key players across the corporation and listen to their opinions, suggestions, and concerns to understand where the corporation wants to go and whether it has the capabilities to get there. During this discovery and research phase, you will likely feel a sense of excitement and a desire to produce results while the ideas are fresh. However, take the time to gather all sentiments across the enterprise to ensure that what you hear on one side of the organization is echoed on the other.

Furthermore, some can get caught up in the "buzz" of Agile. Jennifer Morelli, Principal at Grant Thornton, sees this often and cautions clients to not get snared by it. She challenges her clients by asking questions similar to those stated earlier: "What are you trying to specifically accomplish? What value are you trying to realize?" The underlying objectives are what matter: "Set the right objectives up front, then you can work toward them. Undertaking an Agile transformation without set objectives, just so you can say you have an Agile organization? That's not enough."

> "Set the right objectives up front, then you can work toward them. Undertaking an Agile transformation without set objectives, just so you can say you have an Agile organization? That's not enough."
>
> **Jennifer Morelli**, *Grant Thornton*

When determining your corporation's transformational approach, keep Morelli's advice in mind: transformations are a means to the end, not the ends unto themselves. They are the proverbial tools in the toolkit. Don't focus your corporation on "doing Agile" or "doing Lean" or "doing automation." Instead, focus on meeting your strategic objectives. The mechanisms to get there may rightfully include Agile, Lean, or other approaches, but with the aid of your team and trusted advisors, that's for you to decide.

Spotlight

Finding the Right Path

Gilli Aliotti
CBS Interactive, VP, Project Management

An accomplished senior executive and thought leader with twenty-five successful years across multiple industries including media, entertainment, IT, and education, Gilli Aliotti has led several large-scale Agile transformations at global corporations like CBS Interactive, the Walt Disney Company, Yahoo! Inc., among many others.

Through her extensive experience leading these transformations, Aliotti has found that leaders must first take the time to understand the unique objectives of their businesses. This step is often deprioritized, or even neglected, as corporations race to match their competitors through "buzz" topics like Agile, leading to less than ideal outcomes. Instead, corporations need to understand their goals and pressure test whether these goals align with the outcomes of Agile before undertaking an Agile transformation.

To help corporations set themselves up for a successful transformation, Aliotti asks fundamental questions to help understand their underlying business needs. The first and most important is, "What is the corporation actually trying to achieve?" If leaders are just looking for increased productivity or better collaboration, it's very possible that there are other paths more suitable to the situation that don't include Agile. Another question is, "What are the current pain points?" Pain points that have little to do with the benefits of Agile would indicate that the company should consider a different approach.

Regardless of the specific questions Aliotti asks, the underlying theme remains the same: leaders must start with the basics and understand the business problem, challenges, and potential opportunities before engaging in a transformation of any sort. Aliotti adds, "Agile can be an effective means to help solve these problems, meet the challenges, and act on the potential opportunities, but it is not the end of the road. Used improperly or unnecessarily, Agile won't be any better than your current way of working."

Is Agile the Answer?

Understand what Agile can do for your enterprise and
ask yourself: "Is this right for us?"

Once you are clear about your corporation's strategic objectives and operating model, you can then determine whether Agile is right for you. Make no mistake, Agile is a powerful approach, capable of delivering tremendous business value when utilized correctly. However, when mismatched with an enterprise's objectives, it can leave much to be desired, producing unnecessary overhead and waste. To decide if Agile is right for you, first understand what you can realize by being agile. Many will attribute traits like quality and customer focus to Agile. Others will hail Agile as a path to perfect one's culture. And, while these aren't necessarily wrong, one can definitely be more focused. To illustrate, when you have truly achieved corporate agility, you can expect four characteristics: adaptive, collaborative, rapid, and transparent.

Once you understand what Agile can do for your enterprise, ask yourself: "Does this align with my desired operating model?" Often, the

Corporate Agility Characteristics

Based on corporate success stories and executive interviews, expect to realize these outcomes upon achieving corporate agility.

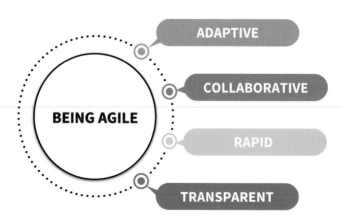

ADAPTIVE

COLLABORATIVE

BEING AGILE

RAPID

TRANSPARENT

Source: DayBlink, 2020

Spotlight

Agile in the Corporation

Elaine Stone
Capital One, Director, Agile Portfolio, Consumer Identity

"**B**e thoughtful in your strategic approach. Ensure your efforts tie back to the problem you're solving for." Elaine Stone, a focused and driven professional with wide-ranging experiences in operations, Agile methodologies, and process optimization and who has led large-scale Agile transformations at large corporations like Capital One, Verizon Media, and AOL, finds this idea to be particularly pertinent as corporations look to scale Agile across the enterprise.

Through these experiences, Stone has found that these "ties," manifested through metrics, will center around how adaptive and rapid a corporation is as it navigates today's changing environment. "We're working in a dynamic environment. Trends are moving at an accelerating pace and staying ahead of them is critical. Agile can be a means to the end … but is not the end itself." Stone's caveat is an important idea as she finds many teams will over-index on "Agile metrics" like burndown charts, NPS, velocity. And while these metrics can show how well Agile is proliferating, remember Stone's original advice: tie Agile back to what you are trying to solve for in the first place.

Stone finds it helpful to give teams the autonomy to choose their own metrics, provided that the metrics they select align under corporate-wide objectives or key results. "You cannot be prescriptive and say we must do this, or we must do that. But you still need to make sure that the individuals and teams doing the work are aligned to the fundamental value and what we're trying to drive."

With this approach, Stone has helped her teams at Capital One embrace Agile. And although she suggests that it is especially paramount in larger corporations and scaled Agile settings, Stone wholeheartedly believes that all organizations, no matter the size, can benefit.

exercise is as easy as taking your desired operating model and character-istics within and seeing if they match the characteristics of Agile. For example, if you're looking for a more collaborative environment because having one would directly drive your objectives, consider Agile, as it can provide the engagement to do so.

Sometimes, however, your objectives and Agile may not align. Take, for example, a pharmaceutical company focused singularly on reducing operating costs through decreased variability in their products. Although quality is something one can achieve through Agile, another methodology like Lean or Six Sigma may be more prudent to adopt as little to no emphasis is placed on the other characteristics of Agile. Alternatively, overlay Agile's values and principles with the other methodology. Doing so can lead to myriad benefits, like streamlined adoption and process synergies. As discussed in further detail in Chapter 10, many corporations have found success with this approach as the values and principles of Agile do not necessarily need to describe Agile environments; in fact, one can often apply them in conjunction with non-Agile, even waterfall, ways of working.

"Danger, Will Robinson!"

Account for the costs before deciding whether Agile is
the right fit.

As previously mentioned, when the outcomes of Agile are appropriately married with a corporation's desired operating model and characteristics within, Agile can be a powerful framework or toolkit that supports significant business value realization. That said, there are other supporting considerations that a corporation must acknowledge to ensure they have the capability to embark on the journey in the first place. For example, if your corporation isn't prepared to invest in training initiatives, Agile will be unable to flourish. That said, all considerations should roll up to the following five:

- **Capacity**: How much time and effort can your corporation allocate to transform?
- **Culture**: How open is your corporation to changing its culture?
- **Existing Operations**: How will ongoing operational activities be impacted by a major transformation? Are your current processes compatible with an Agile transformation effort?
- **People**: How receptive are your people, both current and future, to changing roles, responsibilities, and ways of working? How open is leadership to adjusting your workforce to better suit an Agile way of working?
- **Timing**: Are there more pressing matters that the corporation needs to prioritize? Are there external factors, such as a downturn in the economy or a natural disaster, impacting your company's readiness to embark on a major transformation initiative?

If you fail to appropriately acknowledge these considerations, it will be difficult to implement Agile successfully. Instead of the characteristics you were hoping to achieve, you will instead experience unnecessary overhead, waste, and, worse, uninspiring results.

Take, for example, the UK government's welfare reform project, otherwise known as Universal Credit, which failed to account for the time and effort required for an Agile transformation; pushing an over-aggressive timeline led them to incur a £2.4 billion cost.[7] Another example can be found when diagnosing the failure of SIREN, the large-scale IT project delivering a record and case management system through Agile. The project's inability to bring their teams on board and instill Agile processes and structures resulted in a massive failure, costing ~£15 million with nothing to show for it.[8]

The above considerations will inherently include both hard and soft costs. The hard costs are often considered "hidden" or ancillary as, individually, they may be trivial. Just as the benefits of small improvements and wins amass over time, so, too, can costs. Over the course of a transformation, they will likely accumulate into a consequential amount. Examples of such could include using external advisors, investing in learning and development tools, supporting physical co-location, and providing higher salaries as people transition to new and specialized roles. It may also include sunk costs as in-flight projects are reprioritized or outright canceled.

Supporting Considerations for Agility

When determining if Agile is right for your enterprise, focus your assessment around the following considerations.

Source: DayBlink, 2020

Consider opportunity costs as well, for example, the lag time between when you embark on your Agile journey and when you start to realize positive value. Depending on the corporation, the lag time to reach the steady-state characteristics of Agile can be quite long: many estimate the average Agile transformation takes three to five years to realize its full potential.[9] If quick business value must be realized, avoid large-scale transformations; rather, implement Agile within a pilot group (discussed further in Chapter 8) or consider other initiatives, like vendor investments, strategic partnerships, or digital implementations, that

Spotlight

Understand
Your Goals

Susan Marricone
Honeywell, Director, Agility Transformation Leader

Over the years, Susan Marricone has led Agile transformations across various industries, sectors, and geographies, spanning the gamut from small startups to large Fortune 500 companies. She specializes in ensuring strategic alignment and operational excellence, setting corporations up for success as they embark on their Agile journeys.

In Marricone's previous experience, corporations will "often rush into their Agile transformations, jumping into multi-year initiatives without first understanding where they are as an organization" – one of the most crucial steps in the process. Fortunately, through her experience leading strategies that have refocused executive, technology, and business teams and positioned them for success, Marricone has settled on a set of discussion points and questions to ask executives to help corporations choose the right course of action.

She often starts by asking, "Is your organization in the right position to do this?" Agile transformation gets down into the very bones and DNA of an organization and will likely result in a fundamental change in the corporation's culture. As such, these "transformations often require a tremendous amount of time and effort that many organizations, frankly, don't have." Before embarking on an Agile journey, or any transformation for that matter, corporations must ask themselves if this journey and the potential benefits from it justify the amount of disruption that it often causes.

Another question that Marricone asks is "Why do you want to do this and what are you hoping to accomplish?" Sometimes corporate leaders say they want to "do Agile," but upon digging a little deeper, it might turn out their primary goal is for "continuous improvement" or "better innovation." This lack of clarity "will likely create a mismatch between the methodology and the company." These corporations might be better off focusing primarily on building the Agile mindset or adopting the practices that are most closely aligned with the organization's desired outcomes.

often don't involve such a fundamental change and disruption of your enterprise's culture and DNA.

Other sacrifices – "costs" in their own right – will have to be made in order to successfully execute an Agile transformation. As an executive, you may need to accept some discomfiting changes, particularly with regard to a reduction in executive-level "control." The command-and-control hierarchical ways of operating may need to be exchanged for ones more focused on empowerment and enablement of all people, regardless of position or rank (discussed further in Chapter 6).

As discussed earlier in the chapter, Agile's underlying theme attempts to solve for a business problem that is timeless. The need to deliver working and relevant products in a timely manner will never go away. Similarly, the need to innovate faster than the competition, to foster a positive culture, to hire and develop the best talent will never leave. As such, it's probable that if Agile isn't the right choice for your corporation now, it will be at some point down the road when strategic alignment is greater or when corporation capabilities are more refined to accept an Agile way of working. When that time comes, be prepared to utilize Agile to its fullest extent. Be committed to the journey. With that said, before you learn about how to implement Agile across your corporation, first understand the different worlds and options of Agile.

CHAPTER 3

The Time for Agile?

Agile can be thought of in two different ways – the values and principles that enable the characteristics of Agile and the structures and processes that inform an Agile way of working. Understand both in the pursuit of corporate agility.

The Foundation of Agile

Understand how the values and principles of Agile
enable your corporation to be agile.

Agile is both about being agile and doing Agile. Being agile (also referred to
as lowercase-a agile) is about internalizing the values and principles of Agile
and demonstrating, in words and actions, the characteristics most often
associated with Agile: adaptable, collaborative, rapid, and transparent.
Doing Agile (also referred to as capital-A Agile), on the other hand, refers to
finding ways of working that align with Agile values and principles – your
Agile approach – to achieve your objectives. Your Agile approach should
be informed by the various Agile implementation frameworks and toolkits
that have gained popularity and have been used by others. The decision to
use a standard or hybrid Agile approach must be made with your eyes wide
open. In this chapter, you'll find guidance to help you make that decision.

Doing Agile vs. Being agile

There are two components of Agile, both important in achieving corporate agility.

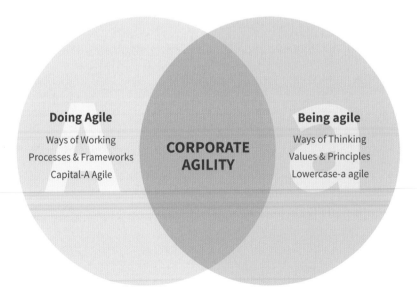

Doing Agile
Ways of Working
Processes & Frameworks
Capital-A Agile

CORPORATE AGILITY

Being agile
Ways of Thinking
Values & Principles
Lowercase-a agile

Source: Data from Prosci, Accessed 2020[1]

It's important to note that the principles underlying Agile were put in practice well before they were formalized in the Agile Manifesto. For example, Kent Beck's Extreme Programming (XP), Jeff Sutherland's Scrum, and many other process-oriented frameworks arose in the 1970s and 1980s with themes similar to that of Agile. Beck, Sutherland, and others recognized, however, the need to unify under a single way of thinking. This led to the famous 2001 Utah meeting where the Agile Manifesto was created, gathering these precepts under the Agile umbrella. These, predominantly United States–based, seventeen computer programmers standardized the Agile tenants, which have grown over decades.

While the Agile Manifesto was originally meant to improve the work of small to mid-sized software development teams, it has, over time, been used with much success across teams and enterprises of all manner and sizes. Its values and principles have been applied to settings well beyond anything envisioned by its creators. No matter which organization or department you work in, the values, principles, and ways of working promulgated by Agile will likely provide significant benefits to your corporation.

For most agilists, the values of the manifesto are lived every day and don't necessitate inclusion herein. But since many are still early into, or haven't launched, their personal or corporate Agile journey, it's important to start at the beginning. Level setting on the heart of Agile and the intent of the Agile Manifesto co-authors – to be agile – is important. Understanding only the superficial list is not enough.

Agile Manifesto Values

The four values of Agile identified by the co-authors of the Agile Manifesto.

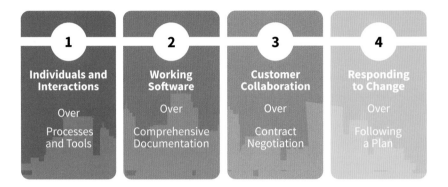

1	**2**	**3**	**4**
Individuals and Interactions	**Working Software**	**Customer Collaboration**	**Responding to Change**
Over	Over	Over	Over
Processes and Tools	Comprehensive Documentation	Contract Negotiation	Following a Plan

Source: Adapted from Agile Manifesto, 2001[2]

As mentioned, most experienced agilists live the values of the manifesto. These values are internalized and guide both how they think and how they work in Agile. On your personal journey to corporate agility, strive to do the same. Empower your team and your corporation to embody the four values. Doing so, you will find that the frameworks, toolkits and processes that many believe wholly represent Agile, while still important, are a mere veneer over what being agile truly means. As you read through the four Agile values, you'll find that they are neither new nor unique to today; rather, they are themes that adaptive, collaborative, rapid, and transparent teams have used to realize their version of corporate agility throughout human history.

1   Individuals and interactions over processes and tools

People drive business value while processes and tools only support them in doing so. Ensure your teams can succeed by prioritizing effective communication and fostering the one-team culture. Furthermore, emphasize flexibility in lieu of rigid Agile structures, processes, or tools. In doing so, you will enable and proliferate Agile's people-first approach to getting work done.

2   Working software over comprehensive documentation

Working products are the right products. Don't avoid documentation altogether; rather, be smart by creating and using documents
that help drive Agile's underlying theme: get relevant and working
products into the hands of the customer. Too much planning and
documenting of product features, some of which may never get
used, results in wasted time.

3   Customer collaboration over contract negotiation

Teams and customers who collaborate are more likely to
succeed. Rarely will an original contract define what a customer
ultimately needs. As such, teams must work alongside their clients,
communicating continuously and frequently to develop the product
or service that they want. This will also work to build stronger
relationships between teams and their customers.

4   Responding to change over following a plan

The world is continuously changing; those who adapt alongside
those changes will succeed. To follow suit, encourage flexibility and
openness to change, and deliver the products and services that are
relevant and work. Agile's iterative approach inherently provides
opportunities to evaluate and adjust to accommodate changes in
the market, customer preferences, or stakeholder priorities.

AGILE PRINCIPLES
AS STATED IN THE AGILE MANIFESTO

1 Our highest priority is to satisfy the customer through early and continuous delivery of valuable software.

2 Welcome changing requirements, even late in development. Agile processes harness change for the customer's competitive advantage.

3 Deliver working software frequently, from a couple of weeks to a couple of months, with a preference to the shorter timescale.

4 Business people and developers must work together daily throughout the project.

5 Build projects around motivated individuals. Give them the environment and support they need, and trust them to get the job done.

6 The most efficient and effective method of conveying information to and within a development team is face-to-face conversation.

Source: Adapted from Agile Manifesto, 2001[1]

In addition to the Agile Manifesto's four values, the co-authors also established twelve supporting principles to guide actionable means of enabling those values. While the values are the foundational ideals to live by, the principles are the means to execute against them. Each principle can be used to pressure test whether you're truly embracing Agile. That said, in an effort to provide flexible guidelines instead of strict rules, each of the following principles were not taken verbatim from the Agile Manifesto. Rather, they have been reworded to align better with general actionable advice that can be tailored for your corporation.

1   Satisfy the customer through early and continuous delivery of valuable software.

Deliver high-quality products and services rapidly and gather continual product feedback. Through this continuous delivery model teams are able to regularly adapt and update products and services, maintaining customers' attention and consistently meeting new demands and

7. Working software is the primary measure of progress.

8. Agile processes promote sustainable development. The sponsors, developers, and users should be able to maintain a constant pace indefinitely.

9. Continuous attention to technical excellence and good design enhances agility.

10. Simplicity – the art of maximizing the amount of work not done – is essential.

11. The best architectures, requirements, and designs emerge from self-organizing teams.

12. At regular intervals, the team reflects on how to become more effective, then tunes and adjusts its behavior accordingly.

expectations. By operating with a mindset of "never having a perfect product," your enterprise can continue to push the envelope, creating incremental product improvements and driving continuous value.

2 Welcome changing requirements, even in late development.

Be nimble and adaptable on short notice. Adapt your priorities to match changes in the market, customer preferences, or stakeholder priorities. Take each change as an opportunity for your business to push itself. By doing so you will maximize value to the customer, rather than deliver a product that falls short of expectations, has become outdated, or is no longer needed.

3 Deliver working software frequently.

Prioritize speed and frequency. Abandon long cycle times in favor of short time-boxed iterations. As the market changes at an ever-faster rate, the pressure to keep up with new trends and keep customers happy and loyal continues to mount. By condensing product delivery timelines, and regularly iterating on any shortcomings of active products, companies are able to better meet the ever-changing demands of their consumers.

4 Prioritize close, daily cooperation between business people and developers.

Have open and clear communication between the working team and key stakeholders. A group of skilled individuals alone will not deliver a quality product; the team and stakeholders need to collaborate and work together as a cohesive unit. Frequent and direct communication with stakeholders is key to understanding changing business needs as soon as possible, minimizing wasted effort on a product or service that is not aligned with stakeholders' expectations.

5 Build projects around motivated individuals.

Staff projects and initiatives with dedicated and motivated people who understand and believe in the product vision. Motivation is a powerful attribute that can inspire others to follow suit, contributing to the success of the initiative as a whole. Furthermore, it can enable autonomous teams, allowing them to focus on incremental product improvements, resulting in higher caliber products.

6 Consider face-to-face conversation as the most effective method of conveying information.

In-person interactions are inherently stronger and more time-sensitive than non-face-to-face conversations. They allow individuals to assess body language, tone, and attitude, making it less likely that a message or conversation will be interpreted incorrectly. Furthermore, having strong communication will foster a more synergistic work environment, inspiring a more impactful team. It's important to note, however, with the advent of technology, virtual face-to-face communication is increasingly effective and something to watch out for (discussed further in Chapter 11).

7   **Measure progress primarily through working software.**

Prioritize getting working products to customers. This principle ties in with Agile's second value. If months and months are spent on requirements and design, no value and, thus, no progress is actually achieved. Agile is about getting feedback swiftly and early. Stakeholders and customers will be unable to provide feedback if the product cannot be tested. Instead, by measuring delivery of functional and working products, you truly are able to evaluate your production success.

8   **Utilize Agile processes to sustain a constant development pace.**

Set a cadence and hold yourself and your team accountable for meeting it. In doing so, teams are more likely to see success in reaching their goals without having to face crunch times. Furthermore, sustaining a predictable development pace will make you a reliable partner in the eyes of the customer, creating a stronger business relationship. Make sure goals are challenging, but achievable – the positive reinforcement that results from completing tasks on time will boost team morale, generating higher productivity.

9   **Enhance agility through continuous attention to technical excellence and good design.**

Continuously learn and strive for technical excellence, enabling teams to understand the different ways and methods to solve problems. In doing so, teams will be able to pick and choose the method that satisfies the customers' needs simply and efficiently. Furthermore, focusing on good design allows teams to develop the functional products that customers actually want, deprioritizing the niceties that may not add value.

10 **Maximize simplicity by limiting the amount of work not done.**

Be efficient. Prioritize and deliver functionalities of your product or service that matter. Oftentimes, the end user will not use some features; ensure you are identifying the ones they will. Furthermore, reduce time spent on non-value-add processes – excessive documentation, manual reporting, meetings – in favor of work that drives principle three: working products. Prioritizing this way of working enables your teams to "work smarter, not harder."

11 **Understand that the best architectures, requirements, and designs emerge from self-organizing teams.**

Enable autonomous teams with a flatter organizational structure. Pushing decisions out to the entire team empowers everyone to collaborate and own the work (this assumes a culture of Individualism; global cultural implications are explored in Chapter 6). As such, team members will be more committed to spot issues, improve the work, and do whatever it takes to see the product succeed in the end. A large misconception, however, is that teams are not able to turn to one person on the team to make certain decisions. Understand that the team is still self-organized if the decision is autonomous and mutual.

12 **Reflect on how to become more effective at regular intervals, then fine tune and adjust behavior accordingly.**

Assess and continuously improve yourself and your teams. As change inevitably occurs, respond to it promptly (as discussed in manifesto value four). The number-one mistake any team can make is to fail and not learn from the failure. Ensure you internalize why something went wrong, and apply it to the next iteration. In doing so, your teams will be empowered to improve incrementally.

At the end of the day, understanding and internalizing these values and principles is what empowers your teams and your corporation to truly be Agile. And, while the frameworks, toolkits, processes, and structures discussed in the next section enable you to do Agile, without the values and principles to accompany them, you'll find it quite hard to realize the team and enterprise characteristics you had hoped to achieve: adaptable, collaborative, rapid, and transparent. Take, for example, a failed Agile initiative: the initial launch of Healthcare.gov. On the surface, the development team was working in an Agile manner; however, dig a little deeper and you'll find that such was not the case.

Case Study: Healthcare.gov

Healthcare.gov was originally created in 2013 to act as the official health care exchange, allowing Americans to compare and enroll in health care plans, among other functionalities. During the first week of launch, however, less than 1% of the eight million visitors were able to use the site properly.[4] In fact, it's reported that only a total of six users were able to complete and submit applications on the first day.[5] It's no surprise, then, that the rollout was considered a massive failure and Agile took part of the blame.

There is much speculation about the true underlying causes of the website failure. Some suggest that the employees and managers had a lack of technical experience; others attribute it to a lack of leadership or formal division of responsibilities between those involved.[6] Many, however, agree with software manager and author Bishr Tabbaa, who points out that the development team's ways of working resembled that of fake Agile: when teams work and adhere to Agile frameworks and toolkits without truly embracing an Agile way of thinking.

He explains: "…some of the component teams refined the UX through wireframes, worked in Sprints, and published code on Github, [but these] were a glossy veneer around the Waterfall process that stacked component construction in parallel and delayed integration testing until the end."[7] Tabbaa identifies a great point; although the teams used an Agile framework, they lacked true commitment to the values and principles of Agile (for example, creating working products). As such, testing the website to ensure functionality was pushed out and only

Spotlight

Achieving Success by Being Agile

Marcus Johnson
Highmark Health, SVP, Enterprise Effectiveness

As a seasoned executive, Marcus Johnson is known for driving financial and operational excellence through large-scale business transformation. Through his years at Deloitte Consulting and other leading organizations, advising strategic execution and large-scale transformations, Johnson has found that "while, for any given way of working the processes and structures are important, what is arguably most critical are the behaviors and values."

Johnson found this to be true first-hand at Highmark Health, the second largest integrated delivery and financing system (IDFS) in America. At the time, Highmark was experiencing tremendous success utilizing Agile in pockets across the enterprise. However, as Johnson and other leaders looked to scale the initiative, they found "if a process or framework works well for a certain individual or team, that does not necessarily mean it will work for others."

As such, Highmark began framing Agile in two distinct ways: doing Agile and being agile. While the former is standing up formal Agile teams and adhering to a particular framework, the latter is a more flexible approach: "empowering teams to embody the values, mindsets, and behaviors of Agile." These teams may utilize a "fail fast, fail often" approach, prioritize the needs of the customer, or slice and sequence work as a means to be more efficient, among other behaviors intrinsic to Agile without its formal structures. This flexible approach recognizes that Scrum, or any of the other Agile frameworks, may not work for every team. What is applicable to all, however, are the themes that underscore Agile.

With this mindset, Johnson entrusts teams at Highmark to find the approach that works for them, whether it is a formalized construct of Agile or an embodiment of its values and principles. As a result of this approach, Highmark has realized success scaling Agile across the enterprise as it works to transform modern healthcare across America.

conducted just days before the first launch, a now-evident precursor to the failed launch of Healthcare.gov.[8]

This failure exemplifies the pitfalls that can occur when lacking a true adoption of Agile, an Agile way of thinking. As with Lean, Six Sigma, or any other methodology, doing Agile for the sake of appearance is not the path to success. Be wary of fake Agile, as it can and will likely inhibit your teams from achieving true Agile success.

Trust Your Gut – If You Don't Feel It, Don't Do It

For Agile to succeed, you really need to believe it. Then, you can champion the change you want to see.

Much of the content in this book thus far has probably come off as analytical or perhaps academic, and it would be misleading to say there isn't more to come. That's because implementing Agile requires this mindset: understanding and utilizing the data to deal with the timeless challenges you face today, and will continue to face in the future. With that said, facts can only provide so much direction. No one can convince you to truly believe in the values and principles of Agile – you need to find your way there, by reading, by learning, and, ultimately, by being and doing. If you don't truly believe, could you possibly convince others to embark upon an Agile journey?

To illustrate, let's return to the analogy from Chapter 2 that compared a runner's path to that of your corporation's: a world-class distance runner wants to train in a particular way to develop specific characteristics necessary to run a marathon. This approach is akin to how your corporation wants to implement Agile to attain a desired operating model, and characteristics within, to realize your strategic objectives. But how do you get a world-class runner to start running in the first place?

That runner requires a coach, a mentor, or a leader, someone who's championing the runner to succeed and will do what it takes to ensure it

Spotlight

Collective Vision and Agile Alignment

Anthony Olsen
Windstream Enterprise, Product Owner

When Broadview Networks merged with Windstream Communications in 2017, Anthony Olsen, along with other leaders at the company, helped drive a transformation from a traditional, waterfall way of working, to a lightweight, Agile one. He attributes a majority of the efficiency and effectiveness of the transition to the corporation's ability to foster a collective vision that drove a true cultural shift and a change in how people collaborated.

This Agile alignment was driven mostly by the company's vision, spearheaded by CEO Tony Thomas. Thomas envisioned Agile creating more business value for customers and better day-to-day operations for his team members. This vision was communicated at quarterly town hall meetings and through various mediums, including internal social media posts.

Thomas has been and continues to be very active on Stream, the company's internal social collaboration platform, and Olsen believes that Thomas's dedication to interacting closely and genuinely with all of Windstream's employees, irrespective of level or rank, is what drove a true alignment on the Agile vision. His personal commitment to, and belief in, these on-the-ground interactions would further proliferate to other leaders and executives, empowering them to follow in step. As Olsen puts it, "Agile was successful [at Windstream] because our leaders supported and engaged on the ground."

Another facet that helped the corporation's collective Agile alignment was the widespread action of listening. Olsen's teams understood Agile to be a framework, not a rulebook that mandated activities for each team member. As such, they made sure to maintain open lines of communication and mutual trust to work toward a common goal. For example, when some members voiced that they were "bombarded with meetings," everyone involved worked to ensure that this problem was heard, recognized, and solved. This aligned Agile transformation has resulted in continued success for Olsen, his teams, and Windstream overall.

happens, through all the ups and downs. Similarly, your corporation and your teams need someone to lead from above who is excited about Agile and determined for its success in the enterprise. You must become that leader: your transformation will not succeed unless you believe, in your gut, that Agile is right for your corporation.

This is not to say, however, that you can just will such a belief into existence. As such, return back to the beginning of this chapter. You already know that Agile can help your corporation achieve its strategic objectives (explored in Chapter 2). Instead, read the values and principles once more and ask yourself, "Is this who I truly want to be?" If it is, congratulations! You've already overcome one of the many reasons why Agile transformations can fail – a lack of executive buy-in. Now, for the easier part.

Embarking on Your Agile Journey

Find the Agile approach that will work for you.

Team structures, processes, and practices can vary widely depending on your Agile approach. There are numerous popular and well-marketed Agile frameworks and toolkits, most of which can be categorized into one of two buckets: standard (pre-established Agile ways of working) and hybrid frameworks (pre-established combinations of two or more Agile or non-Agile methodologies). No matter the framework or toolkit, you will need to tailor aspects of the approach to better fit the unique and distinct needs of your corporation.

To illustrate, consider this analogy: say your corporation is looking for a new suit and while, sometimes, an off-the-rack suit fits perfectly, more often than not, alterations are needed. The same concept applies for Agile – an available framework or toolkit must be altered to meet the needs of your corporation. Additionally, while there are many different suits available, there are some common trusted brands. Once again, Agile is no different. There are a few common starting points that are well known in the community: Scrum@Scale, Kanban, Disciplined Agile (DA), and Scaled Agile Framework (SAFe). The Agile Manifesto's values and principles are embodied in each of these frameworks in a unique way, and while there is no right or wrong approach, choose one that is most compatible with your teams and your corporation – culture, team size, corporation size, technical practices, organizational type, industry.

Find Your Unique Framework

Choose a standard or hybrid framework as your starting point, then continuously evolve it to fit your corporation.

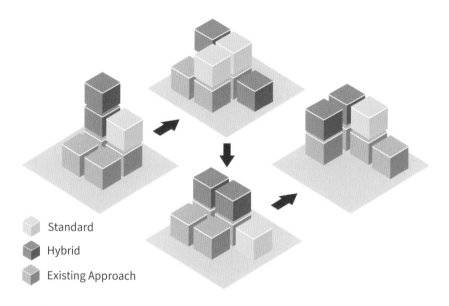

Standard

Hybrid

Existing Approach

Source: DayBlink, 2020

Furthermore, be flexible with the implementation of your Agile approach. Sometimes, you may discover, partway through your implementation, that a different approach would be more effective in your corporation. Be willing to accept this discovery as a setback, learn from it, and iterate (discussed further in Chapter 6). Additionally, you'll find that implementing one framework across the corporation is often not optimal, as different verticals and teams will have different characteristics and, as such, different needs. For example, SAFe could be a good fit for the IT department while Scrum might be more effective for Finance. Again, find the right approach that works for you.

Scrum@Scale

	FOUNDER	Jeff Sutherland
SCRUM @SCALE	FOUNDED	2018
	URL	www.scrumatscale.com

Source: Adapted from Jeff Sutherland, 2020[?]

Scrum is often the first framework that comes to mind when people think of Agile. At its core, Scrum is a process model that describes how teams should plan, update, and analyze their work. To work in Scrum, start by taking your overall product or solution and decomposing it into smaller increments until they become user stories, the smallest unit of work that provides customer value. Then, teams complete these user stories in priority order over the course of a Sprint, building incrementally toward the end product or solution.

Scrum uses the time-boxed nature of a Sprint to hold teams accountable for the work delivered at the end of each Sprint, popularly known as the product increment. By having such a structure, the Scrum framework encourages an iterative delivery process where the team can receive feedback from the stakeholders at scheduled review sessions, as well as throughout the development process.

Launched in 2018, Scrum@Scale builds upon and extends the original Scrum framework to tens, hundreds, and even thousands of teams throughout an Agile operating system. It solves for the major challenges of scaling Agile – decreased volume, speed, and quality, and misaligned management structure – by focusing on two specific elements, as outlined by the Scrum@Scale guide:[10]

- **Linear Scalability**: Ensuring a corresponding increase in delivery of product with an increase in teams
- **Business Agility**: Prioritizing the ability to rapidly respond to change by adapting its initial stable configuration

To implement Scrum@Scale, be aware of a few considerations. First, ensure that you are familiar with the original Scrum framework. As the Scrum@Scale guide says, "If an organization cannot Scrum, it cannot scale."[11] Also, ensure that your organization is standardized on terminology and processes to streamline the rollout. Steve Elliott, head of Jira Align at Atlassian, underscores this sentiment: "When scaling, it can be beneficial to implement certain guardrails. This means having a bit of commonality across the organization, and agreeing to do certain things, certain ways." While this is not to say that each team must be a carbon copy of the other, it does emphasize the importance of having centralized processes, structures, and purpose. If teams are not working together toward the same true North, the enterprise is unlikely to scale Agile successfully.

> "When scaling, it can be beneficial to implement certain guardrails. This means having a bit of commonality across the organization, and agreeing to do certain things, certain ways."
>
> **Steve Elliott**, *Atlassian*

As discussed in their 2014 book, *Scrum: The Art of Doing Twice the Work in Half the Time*, Jeff and JJ Sutherland emphasize the impact Scrum and Scrum@Scale can have on a company when it comes to fostering a cooperative workplace: "Scrum emphasizes transparency to build trust and commitment."[12] This transparency allows team members to feel comfortable around each other, empowering them to ask hard questions, challenge the norm, and push for greater products.

This team interaction, in conjunction with Agile's prioritization of quick and iterative delivery, can create tremendous results. Take, for example, one of the most prominent Scrum@Scale case studies: 3M. They had used Scrum@Scale to scale their initial Agile practice to an astounding three-hundred cross-functional teams. Critical success factors included better backlog refinement, limiting meetings to five people to speed up decision time, and rotating Product Owners, Scrum Masters, and team members. In the end, 3M scaled Agile to over 1500 staff and the number continues to climb. In that same time period, their stock price climbed from $84 to $149 billion.[13]

When deciding on the best starting point for your corporation, consider the strengths and drawbacks of a framework. While Scrum and Scrum@Scale enable prompt and continuous delivery and improve the ability to meet customer demands, there are limitations to leveraging these frameworks. For example, while Scrum operates optimally with team sizes of three to nine, Scrum@Scale emphasizes that teams should not be more than five. Jeff Sutherland, the creator of both frameworks, emphasizes this critical point: "Experiments with high-performing Scrum teams have repeatedly shown that four or five people doing the work is the optimal size. It is essential to linear scalability that this pattern be the same for the number of teams in a [Scrum@Scale]." As such, if your teams and the work they are doing necessitates team sizes more than five, it may be prudent to deprioritize Scrum@Scale in lieu of other frameworks.

In addition to team size, understand that Scrum@Scale will require significant effort and time to implement to scale. This applies to all Agile implementations, but as Scrum@Scale is geared toward scaling across entire organizations, the capacity needed cannot be understated. With that said, if Scrum@Scale is implemented correctly, it promises to reap significant benefits for the corporation. Remember, though, Scrum and Scrum@Scale are just two of the many suits on the rack – there might be others that fit better.

Kanban

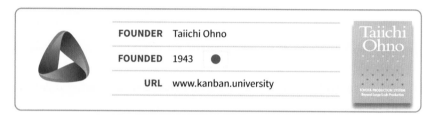

FOUNDER	Taiichi Ohno
FOUNDED	1943 ●
URL	www.kanban.university

Kanban is a visual, workflow management method originally developed by Taiichi Ohno in the 1940s.[15] Kanban's name, meaning "visual signal," alludes to its use of physical or virtual "cards" that are moved on a Kanban "board," representing how work moves through a process from start to finish.[16] While initially developed for the manufacturing floor, it has evolved to penetrate other verticals and industries. Today, Kanban's ability to embrace constant change and engage cross-department collaboration, while ensuring efficiency and quality production, has garnered favorability among many.[17] To achieve these outcomes, Kanban emphasizes four key principles:

- **Visualize Workflow**: Kanban uses "cards" and "boards" to map how work flows throughout a process. In doing so, you will be able to more easily identify areas of improvement.
- **Limit Work in Progress**: Kanban drives increased efficiency through reduced waste. To achieve this, limit work to only that which was "pulled" or asked for by the customer.
- **Focus on Flow**: This principle emphasizes the importance of flow within your process. Once you've visualized it and limited the work within, focus on ensuring an uninterrupted stream of work.
- **Continuous Improvement**: A main tenet of Kanban and, of course, Agile as well, commit yourself and your teams to constantly identifying additional areas of improvement and acting on them.

Success stories of Kanban span the world, from manufacturing plants in Japan to hospitals in Indonesia. Take, as an example, GE Aviation, a subsidiary of General Electric and one of the top aircraft engine suppliers. Using a modified Kanban framework, they were able to define value through the client's eyes and deliver it successfully. They were also able to map their workflow and easily identify bottlenecks and improvement points because of it. In the end, GE Aviation found that the productivity of one person post-implementation was that of three people beforehand![18] While many corporations have found success using Kanban, it may not be compatible with every enterprise or every team. For example, the Kanban process is best suited for stable, repetitive processes. If your team's work necessitates a process that changes often, Kanban may not be the answer. Furthermore, Kanban is often criticized for lacking timeframes within the process. If your teams align with the time-boxed nature of other Agile frameworks, it may be prudent to use those instead.

Disciplined Agile

Disciplined Agile (DA) is an Agile toolkit that pulls from parts of Scrum, Kanban, SAFe, and many others. DA relies on a risk-value delivery life cycle, which is made up of streamlined phases, prioritizing sophisticated work and explicit milestones.[20] Initially created for IT management teams, the toolkit has found much success across different departments, company sizes, and industries. Take, for example, Panera Bread, which utilized DA to keep up with its competitors in the food industry by increasing their solution delivery frequency and improving the working relationship between IT and business.[21]

Designing
Disciplined Agile (DA)

Scott Ambler
Disciplined Agile, Co-Founder
Project Management Institute (PMI), VP

Scott Ambler, a thought leader in the Agile space with over twenty years of Agile experience, has contributed a tremendous amount to the Agile space and community, including authoring several Agile books – *Choose Your WoW!* and *Agile Modeling*, among many others. However, Ambler is best known as co-founder of Disciplined Agile (DA), now a mainstream toolkit helping corporations achieve Agile success.

Ambler's journey started in the mid-1990s, when he first helped corporations implement Agile leveraging standard approaches like Scrum and Kanban. He found, however, that many of his clients struggled to follow these frameworks successfully and, at the time, no one could articulate "why." Similarly, Ambler observed that "those who did find success with Agile couldn't explain how they achieved it," either.

Through this experience, Ambler would come to two overarching conclusions. The first is that "there was a need for some kind of centralized framework or steps to take as everybody was missing the same basic lessons that Scrum, or any other framework, failed to teach." At the same time, however, this toolkit needed to be flexible as every individual, team, and corporation is unique, and will, consequently, have different choices to consider and decisions to make, driving a different Agile journey entirely.

Based on these conclusions, Ambler created Financial Delivery, which later became Disciplined Agile. In 2012, Ambler published his first formal book on the toolkit, which has since become a massive success in the Agile community primarily due to its ability to solve for the two conclusions discussed earlier. "Disciplined Agile is not a framework that dictates how a team should utilize Agile. Instead, it is a flexible toolkit that utilizes many different Agile practices, presenting teams with a wealth of options and guiding them to the correct choice."

Another example can be found in Barclays Bank, which utilized DA to help improve corporate flexibility and nurture a goal-based mentality. By achieving increased throughput and reduced code complexity and deployment cycles, their DA implementation was easily classified a success.[22] The potential DA outcomes are plentiful, but one of the most discussed benefits is its ability to address all aspects of solution delivery, including technical expertise and documentation strategies. By having such an exhaustive capability, teams and enterprises are better able to achieve the business outcomes that Panera Bread and Barclays Bank realized.

Although a powerful toolkit that offers unique benefits, DA is, at the end of the day, a niche one, which comes with certain drawbacks. For example, DA has a lower number of documented case studies when compared to other, more prominent frameworks and toolkits. With fewer examples to emulate, corporations may fail more often and have a tougher time analyzing those failures – a necessary step, as discussed in Chapter 6, for all Agile transformations. Furthermore, the niche character of DA exemplifies the notion that experienced coaches and consultants who can often help drive the implementation processes might be harder to come by. This limitation, in conjunction with the certification dilemma that plagues the Agile community (discussed further in Chapter 7), means that the implementation process may be harder for some teams and corporations.

As mentioned, DA is a hybrid approach, giving corporations the option to flex "levers" and leverage aspects of one framework or toolkit over another. Scott Ambler, co-founder of the DA toolkit, further describes this sentiment: "Because everyone is unique and they face unique situations, you have to give them options and give them the guidance to help them choose the right one." There is obviously a tradeoff, though: corporations not as familiar with Agile or implementing Agile may have a harder time utilizing such a flexible toolkit.

> "Because everyone is unique and they face unique situations, you have to give them options and give them the guidance to help them choose the right one."
>
> **Scott Ambler**, *Disciplined Agile*

Scaled Agile Framework (SAFe)

FOUNDER	Dean Leffingwell	
FOUNDED	2011	
URL	scaledagileframework.com	

Source: Adapted from Dean Leffingwell, Accessed 2020[23]

SAFe quickly became one of the most popular scaled frameworks, typically used by larger, more complex organizations. This does not mean, however, that SAFe's use cases are reserved only for these larger corporations; rather, it can be used across a variety of departments, company sizes, and industries. Part of why SAFe has become so popular is its flexibility and comprehensiveness. SAFe provides four different configurations so that no matter what type of team structure or processes your enterprise already has, there's a decent chance that SAFe can be compatible with it. Furthermore, SAFe and the Scaled Agile team are committed to the continuous improvement of the framework. While writing and publishing this book, SAFe, true to Agile, had iterated itself five times. By the time you read this, there will have definitely been more iterations!

To be so effective, SAFe leverages Agile Release Trains (ARTs), a process in which products, services, or functions are released with a continuous flow of value. This flow allows for errors to be caught and iterations to be made in a timely manner, ensuring the release of quality products into the market rapidly and efficiently. The SAFe framework comes with many proven successes, a clear path to implementation, and a significant amount of training resources for enterprises to leverage. To illustrate a success story, look at Cisco and their Agile journey. By utilizing a SAFe methodology, they saw a 40% decrease in product defects.[24] Air France KLM realized a similar storyline: the teams that used the SAFe framework delivered products 20% more effectively than their waterfall counterparts.[25]

SAFe, as with all of the other frameworks discussed, has certain limitations to consider. For example, SAFe's thoroughness and, sometimes, heavy planning structure may occasionally contradict the original values and principles of the Agile Manifesto. To illustrate further, take the different levels in which teams work under SAFe – the team level, program level, solution level, and portfolio level. As products progress through each of these levels, there is an inherent shift from a design, build,

Framework and Toolkit Landscape

The current landscape of Agile frameworks and toolkits can vary widely by scalability and complexity.

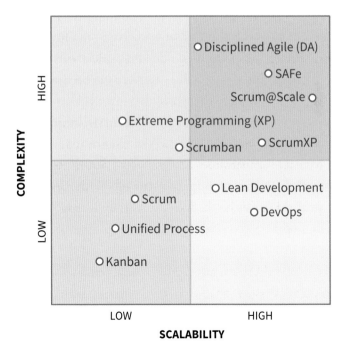

Source: Data from CollabNet VersionOne, 2019[26]

and iterate workplace to a priority setting, theme identifying, and value stream growing environment. Having such an organizational structure limits individuals' ability to be flexible and nimble in comparison with their potential roles in other frameworks.

Ultimately, there are tradeoffs with all Agile frameworks and toolkits, whether standard or hybrid. Whichever framework or toolkit you end up choosing, however, always remember the suit-buying analogy: no "off-the-rack" suit will fit you perfectly. Alter and modify it to become the suit that fits you. The same mindset must be internalized for Agile. Create a unique, tailored framework or toolkit that fits the characteristics and needs of your team and your corporation. Take, for example, the following case study of Spotify, famous for their ability to customize Agile for themselves and see success because of it.

Case Study: Spotify

Spotify employed an Agile methodology in 2008 when the streaming service first launched.[27] Its journey is known today as one of the most prominent case studies of Agile. So much so, that it has had its own framework named after it: the Spotify model. This is because, at Spotify, they had truly internalized how to tailor their approach to their ever-changing needs. It started off with a unique combination of Scrum and Lean, utilizing what they termed "squads," "guilds," and "tribes" to promote innovation.[28] Over the years, their process has continued to evolve as they learn and discover new ways of working.

Henrik Kniberg, the Agile coach who helped champion the original implementation of Agile at Spotify, explains it further: "It wasn't a big re-make, more like a continuous stream of small iterative improvements to our organization and process. We have been growing for three years, and the way we work today has naturally evolved over time." Today, Spotify has 271 million users worldwide, leading the industry, both in revenue and popularity.[29] Though the company has scaled significantly since its 2008 inception, it has kept teams small, scaling the number of teams, not team members, to sustain continuous improvement and Agile operations throughout the corporation.

A great example of how Spotify used its agility to provide customer value is showcased in the company's development of the "Discover Weekly" feature. Spotify received feedback from users detailing the difficulty of finding new songs due to the sheer overwhelming amount of content available. While having a lot of options, especially when it comes to music preferences, is generally considered a good thing, in this case it deterred users from exploring and experiencing new music.

Spotify's solution was its "Discover Weekly" feature, which assesses users' music preferences over a few weeks and then customizes suggestions based on similar artists, styles, and other features. Because of Spotify's organizational structure, which includes little hierarchy or bureaucracy, the design team was able to quickly incept this new feature, receive approval, and turn it into reality. The result was a solution that allowed users to maintain the perks of a vast musical archive while providing unique recommendations that would continuously improve over time. The "Discover Weekly" feature is now one of Spotify's most popular, garnering millions of new users to date.[30] Because of their unique Agile way of working, Spotify was able to innovate, create, and discover a best-in-class solution to give listeners the music they want.

Over time, as you look to develop your own tailored framework or toolkit, be mindful that success is not a given – Agile is not above reproach. Similar to what happened at Healthcare.gov, failure is a very real possibility, but don't let it be a deterrent. Recognize and understand that every organization has failed at some point, in some capacity – although this is not necessarily a bad thing, as discussed in Chapter 6. This is not a phenomenon specific to Agile and is, instead, common across all types of transformations.

Sometimes, by considering your culture, people, capacity, existing operations, and timing, you can overcome some of the common challenges faced in failed transformations. In studying the data of past transformations and the factors that led to their success or failure, however, you'll find that, most of the time, there is another collection of key considerations or lessons to acknowledge as you embark on your corporation's Agile journey.

Spotlight

Be Flexible in
Your Agile Approach

Michael K Sahota
SHIFT314, Speaker, Trainer, & Consultant

Michael Sahota is a preeminent thought leader in the Agile space who helps executives create high-performing organizations. Throughout his twenty years of experience guiding and teaching Agile, Sahota has garnered tremendous distinctions such as his designations as Certified Enterprise Coach (CEC) and Certified Agile Leadership (CAL) Educator, and as author of *An Agile Adoption and Transformation Survival Guide: Working with Organizational Culture* and co-author of *Emotional Science.*

Sahota stresses that "as corporations look to embark on their path to corporate agility, they must remain flexible and adaptive in their approach, something that 95% of transformations fail to do." Instead, leaders will often take a standard framework – Scrum, SAFe, Kanban, etc. – and apply it as a prescriptive, mandated method across the organization without first asking the various individuals and teams, "Does this make sense for you?" Sahota believes this violates a core tenet of Agile: "Agile is about involving people over process."

This is just one of the many ways that Sahota has seen corporations preemptively make decisions, centralizing and standardizing without regard to another one of Agile's core themes: responding to change over following a plan. To solve this, Sahota guides leaders through a fundamental shift in mindset and understanding so they value and feel safe with an emergent Agile approach and the uncertainty that accompanies it: "The moment when leaders define their Agile transformation is the exact moment in which it is not Agile anymore."

Sahota underscores, however, that this does not mean completely ignoring the underlying patterns that have historically made sense. Instead, it means using patterns in a way that is fit-for-purpose and avoids adding to the blocks and distortions in the system that limit performance. Sahota teaches leaders to understand this dichotomy and utilize it to achieve a healthy and natural evolution of an organizational system unique to their corporation.

PART TWO

The Agilessons

[aj-uhl les-uhns] n.

1. How to realize corporate agility and rapidly evolve in the face of accelerating disruption.

2. Unfiltered insights from industry leaders who have lived and thrived through Agile transformations.

CHAPTER 4

An Introduction to the Agilessons

As in life and business, successes and failures abound in Agile as well. It is important to understand what distinguished those who succeeded from those who didn't. Based on discussions with seasoned agilists and executive contributors from around the world, we believe six Agile lessons, or "Agilessons," underpin all successful Agile transformations.

Our Journey

An Agile approach can be powerful when implemented correctly, but quite the opposite when utilized erroneously, driving unnecessary overhead and uninspiring results. As such, it's important to learn what distinguishes those who succeed by using an Agile approach from those who don't. These lessons, or as DayBlink Consulting has termed them, "Agilessons," are a collection of key practices that all executives and corporations can internalize regardless of where they are on their journey and, with careful consideration, can assist anyone in achieving their strategic objectives. As discussed in Chapter 3, to implement Agile successfully, you'll need to determine the approach that best suits you and your corporation. Conforming to this sentiment, these Agilessons are not meant to suggest that there is only one right way to do Agile; in fact, they do quite the opposite. There are infinite nuances and considerations to acknowledge. How we solve for them, however, stays the same.

Agilesson 1: Initiate with Intent

Become an executive sponsor and nurture the one-team culture by instilling the vision of "Why Agile?" Do this by being on the ground and empowering interactions between all team members, regardless of rank or position. Furthermore, ensure your team understands that the transformation will take time and effort and will not happen overnight. Utilize effective communications and flexibility in your scaling approach to circumvent the potential onset of disgruntled or disengaged employees if the adoption of Agile is not what was hoped.

Agilesson 2: Cultivate Your Culture

In Agile, culture is key. Ensure you foster the right one by identifying and leveraging your change champions and top performers, both within and outside the corporation. Then, utilize them to proliferate the culture of trust and fail-fast mentality you'll need to succeed. Finally, understand that your distribution of demographics, in terms of backgrounds and nationalities, may affect how Agile is adopted. Account for this and adjust your approach accordingly.

Agilesson 3: Transform Your Team

Leverage your HR department to identify characteristics of those that will thrive under Agile – adaptive, collaborative, rapid, transparent – and trust in their ability to find them within and outside your corporation. Then, empower your teams to become the workforce of tomorrow: utilize customized learning and development programs, seek out detractors and bring them along on the journey, and help your middle managers transition into their new role under an Agile way of working.

Agilesson 4: Work Wisely

Find ways of working that will enable your teams to thrive. To do this, take the values and principles of the Agile Manifesto in stride. Specifically, prioritize simplicity regarding your documentation and processes, and ensure that your customers' needs are understood and accounted for at all stages of the journey. Furthermore, consider an iterative approach to scaling Agile itself. This Nail and Scale method has found much success by starting Agile small within a pilot group and scaling it, learning along the way. Be aware, however, of the common pitfalls that may arise when undertaking this method of scaling.

Agilesson 5: Measure with Meaning

As a common part of everyday life, metrics can be a powerful tool in gauging your progress toward success, however it's been defined. The translation to a corporate setting is apt. Throughout the course of your implementation journey, answer the three key questions and identify the metrics that can help gauge where you are on your journey toward corporate agility: "How do I know I'm progressing toward strategic objectives?," "How do I know I'm doing Agile?," and "How do I know I'm being agile?" Understand the differences between these questions, and the different metrics they require.

Agilesson 6: Forge Forward

Understand the common trends and behaviors that may indicate Agile has taken root within your corporation. If Agile has become the new normal and this fundamental change in your DNA has occurred, identify other methodologies that can and should coexist with Agile. Similar to Agile, these methodologies are unique and powerful independently. Find the one, or combination, that works for you. Whichever you choose, however, the original lesson is apt: as the world continues to change, and new methodologies come into existence, the underlying themes of Agile are set up to work in conjunction.

In developing these Agilessons, we interfaced with nearly a thousand individuals, gathering information and insights from the Fortune 500, top management consulting firms, and leading agilists. It was truly an ambitious scope and approach. The responses we received, however, were amazing, giving insights into Agile and how companies approach the methodology, not found elsewhere.

The Agilessons were ultimately developed in collaboration with 242 leading Agile practitioners from around the world, representing more than 1,200 years of Agile experience from different industries – hospitality, consumer goods, telecommunications, and private equity – and various corporations – Capital One, Mastercard, and Amazon, among others. In addition to the more than 600 hours spent discussing with, and interviewing, Fortune 500 executives, preeminent thought leaders, and manifesto signatories, another 1,500 hours were spent on primary and secondary research to validate the Agilessons.

When we embarked on this journey five months ago, we hypothesized ten Agilessons. After numerous iterations, in which each Agilesson and the message therein was carefully vetted and considered, we ultimately landed on six Agilessons that collectively exhaust the list of insights one needs to realize corporate agility. These six Agilessons represent the next six chapters, each a deep dive into the Agilesson in question, bolstered by a plethora of examples and data points from the unique stories captured throughout the development of this book.

As discussed earlier in the introduction and a common message throughout the book, these stories are powerful and wholly important to understand why some transformations fail and some succeed. However, what happens in one corporation will not necessarily translate to another. Understand and internalize these insights, but independently assess your corporation and find your unique path to success. To help you do this, you'll find, at the end of each chapter, a retrospective section – a common practice among some of the Agile frameworks and toolkits discussed earlier in this chapter. These sections contain questions to help assess your current situation, topics to initiate, and warning signs to watch out for. When answering these questions, don't compare yourself to others; instead, assess yourself and your corporation to ensure a successful journey to corporate agility. With that said, continue ahead to Chapter 5, Agilesson 1: Initiate with Intent, and take your next step toward continued Agile success!

The Patterns of Agile

Linda Rising
Independent Consultant

As an established author and consultant, with a focus on Agile development and change processes, Linda Rising has made quite the name for herself in the Agile community. Through her extensive experiences, Rising identified some patterns that emerge within corporations embarking on their Agile journey. To help corporations understand and account for these patterns, she later translated them into numerous books, two of which are, *The Patterned Almanac 2000* and *Fearless Change: Patterns for Introducing New Ideas.*

One of the many patterns Rising found is the idea that individuals, teams, and corporations often feel as if Agile lays out a plan and process to follow, a stark contrast to the idea of "responding to change" that is outlined in the Agile Manifesto. To help her clients work through this confusing conundrum, Rising goes through two distinct exercises.

The first is a level setting on the intent of the Agile Manifesto. Rising helps executives understand that Agile does not suggest not following a plan at all, but rather that responding to change should be prioritized over the aforementioned. The second is related to the first. To help corporations respond to change, Rising coaches executives to "implement Agile in small, tiny experiments and learn step by step what works and what doesn't." This allows corporations to be more nimble and able to pivot and adapt if they find their original "plan" was not yielding expected results.

Another particularly interesting pattern Rising noticed is the idea that there are no patterns among Agile transformations. Rising says this facetiously, but not without merit: "All teams and companies are unique, and they will each have a unique Agile journey. What works for one organization will not necessarily work for the next." Rising helps leaders understand this by stressing her original lesson, with an extra caveat: identify and understand common transformation patterns, but also be open to change as you determine your unique path on this Agile journey.

CHAPTER 5

Agilesson 1:

Initiate with Intent

When embarking on your path to corporate agility, ensure to generate the momentum necessary for a successful transformation by instilling an aligned vision and setting realistic expectations.

Journey with the Team

Instill the vision of "Why Agile?" by fostering
the one-team mentality.

If you ask Art Moore, who has years of experience working within
Agile environments, what's necessary for Agile to be successful within
a corporation, he'll tell you, "Agile is top-down and bottom-up. Broad
success is ultimately dependent on leaders who embrace the need for
change, communicate that need downward, and believe in their team
to execute to create business agility." This sentiment shouldn't come as a
surprise. As discussed in Chapter 3, Agile is a "people-first" approach to
getting work done. To enable this workforce, everyone must be brought
along on the journey. As a leader, you must therefore instill a strong sense
of why Agile matters and what it means for your corporation. In doing
so, you'll empower your teams to become the "doers," alluded to by
Moore, and help instill the characteristics of successful transformations.
This idea of coalescing under an aligned vision is further echoed by Walt
Disney: "Of all the things I've done, the most vital is coordinating those
who work with me and aiming their efforts at a certain goal."

> "Agile is top-down and bottom-up. Broad
> success is ultimately dependent on leaders who
> embrace the need for change, communicate
> that need downward, and believe in their team
> to execute to create business agility. "
>
> **Art Moore**, *Clear Systems LLC*

Instilling an aligned vision, however, isn't always a walk in the park.
There will be resistance and there will be challenges. There will be team
members who won't like working in an Agile environment or feel they
are more effective in a traditional one (discussed further in Chapter 7).

Yes, people can adjust, but some habits take longer to break. Sharief Elgamal, a Partner at DayBlink Consulting, describes this resistance: "I believe the biggest impediment is the natural resistance to change. It's a matter of bringing people along on the journey, because people are used to doing things in a certain way, and Agile is different."

To bring your team along and instill your Agile vision, create an environment that fosters the one-team mentality. This does not imply, however, that everyone works in exactly the same way. Rather, it emphasizes a mindset of uniting under an aligned goal. It's about working together as one group, one people, echoing the value underscored in the Agile Manifesto, "Individuals and interactions over processes and tools." Through this mindset, the best team players will support, encourage, and work closely with their teammates. They will set and communicate healthy boundaries and address conflicts as they arise. By growing with their team members, rather than independent of them, they help nurture and further instill the one-team mentality across the corporation.

> "I believe the biggest impediment is the natural resistance to change. It's a matter of bringing people along on the journey, because people are used to doing things in a certain way, and Agile is different."
>
> **Sharief Elgamal**, *DayBlink Consulting*

That said, instilling the one-team mentality doesn't end with finding good team members. You also need to bolster and reinforce it yourself, both in your words and actions. Create mechanisms and processes that ensure there will be opportunities for collaborative interaction between yourself and the teams. Traditionally, people within an organization connect solely with their direct peers or colleagues. With Agile, as alluded to in the manifesto, the goal is for people across different departments, functions, levels, and positions to work together. Jeff Sutherland, Agile

Manifesto signatory and co-creator of Scrum, further underscores this idea: "[Leaders] need to be going right down where the troops are working. They need to be there giving feedback and if they're not, people will not believe that the [leader] wants to be Agile."[1]

Executive Sponsor Traits

Building the one-team culture starts with effective executive sponsorship.

Source: DayBlink, 2020

Establishing these day-to-day interactions can help drive transparency, collaboration, and the one-team mentality necessary for a successful Agile transformation. Take, for example, Telstra Ventures, one of Australia's most valuable companies by market cap and a global top-20 corporate venture capital fund. Telstra was able to achieve corporate agility success because the drive and support came from the very top. Its CEO at the time, David Thodey, was an active role model of the customer-centric and risk-taking mentality he was trying to drive, and championed the change on the ground.[2]

Before instilling your vision, however, understand that there are preexisting societal beliefs about corporate executives, including their mentality and approachability. These beliefs can be challenging to overcome. As such, ensure that you are supportive, engaging with teams over their successes and failures with a servant-leader mentality. Through

Spotlight

One-Team Communication

Allen Broome
MediaKind, CTO

Allen Broome, a technical leader with over twenty-four years of experience, has a proven track record of building and motivating highly productive teams. Through experience holding executive positions at Comcast and MediaKind, Broome has found that of all the responsibilities of an executive there is one that is particularly important in the context of Agile transformation: "enable generative cultures with free-flowing information across the corporation." By executing this responsibility, the one-team mentality is able to proliferate, empowering all team members, regardless of position or rank, to interact, trust, and work together as one toward a common set of goals.

To do this, Broome stresses the importance of having the right processes and tools in place to augment and bolster both the quantity and quality of communications company-wide. By doing so, communication takes place in a consistent and effective way, ensuring the latest information is always available to make the best decisions. However, Broome emphasizes the continued need and importance for leadership to be "on the ground level and engaging teams directly to build the necessary trust and safety for open communication."

Broome also recognizes the importance of adaptability, citing the coronavirus disease (COVID-19) pandemic as an example. As an executive of a global corporation during this crisis, Broome experienced first-hand the need to utilize technology to help his teams adapt to a new and unfamiliar way of working, a sentiment that can also be applied to Agile transformations. He underscores, "With everyone working from home, we need to be able to adapt. To step back, observe, and ask what needs to change to achieve the desired outcomes. But we also need to understand that this need to change is constant, that we'll always have to change to stay relevant and effective."

The importance of providing a constant flow of information through different communication channels is further underscored by the fact that transformations require immense coordination. In order to operate effectively without the normal high degrees of synchronization, teams must be informed with the latest information. Broome stresses that as a leader, "you need to invest the time and energy to not only open these communication channels but allow them to thrive."

this mentality, you are not overseeing your teams, but, instead, supporting and empowering your staff.[3] By doing so, you will enable team members to succeed. Furthermore, by supporting transformations as servant-leaders, you are able to better show how much the teams' efforts are valued, resulting in more empowered and accountable team members. Anthony Olsen, Product Owner at Windstream Enterprise, has seen this first-hand: "Agile was successful because our leaders supported and engaged on the ground, enabling the trust and confidence that we were making the right choices and following the right path."

> "Agile was successful because our leaders supported and engaged on the ground, enabling the trust and confidence that we were making the right choices and following the right path."
>
> **Anthony Olsen**, *Windstream Enterprise*

At the end of the day, instilling an aligned vision will depend greatly on your actions and guidance. Steve Elliott of Atlassian gives astute advice here: "Even if you get some teams interested in doing Agile, and maybe even a product or program, it's hard to drive true transformation without an executive to champion it." Understand this: you must be on the ground to initiate a successful Agile transformation. Journey with your team.

Set Realistic Expectations

Be patient – understand that transformations take time.

As with any transformation effort, your path to deploying Agile within your corporation will take time and effort as long-held practices, processes, and mindsets must be changed. And, although you probably don't need convincing that this time and effort will likely be rewarded in the end, your teams may think otherwise. To mitigate this concern, set realistic expectations. A lack thereof, and you risk disgruntled or disengaged employees when Agile doesn't gain traction in the time period expected or in the amount that they had hoped.

As with other aspects of Agile, the first way to set realistic expectations is through effective communications. Ensure your teams understand this will be a journey with many bumps in the road and that it will take time before benefits are realized, and that's okay. Be honest and unequivocal with them. For those impacted, articulate why you are embarking upon this journey, and point to specific realities that require such dramatic action. As Scott Ambler, co-founder of Disciplined Agile, puts it, "First thing I would say is that the long-term journey is a lot of hard work. And there's no easy answer. So if you're not going in eyes wide open, don't even bother."

Since top-down cultural adoption can often drive transformational success, consider instilling these expectations at the senior levels first. Then, the mindset can cascade down to others. Furthermore, communicate your metrics. As discussed in Chapter 9, metrics are an extremely important part of your Agile journey and can help you and your teams understand, "Is Agile working?" This can be a useful tool, garnering favorability by showing objective progress through data.

> "First thing I would say is that the long-term journey is a lot of hard work. And there's no easy answer. So if you're not going in eyes wide open, don't even bother."
>
> **Scott Ambler**, *Disciplined Agile*

Besides effective communication, consider flexibility in your approach to implementing Agile. Although this will not realign unrealistic expectations, it can help to mitigate the effects of them. To explain further, there are two main approaches to implementing Agile:

Big Bang and Phased approaches. In a nutshell, the Big Bang approach stands up Agile throughout an organization, all at once. A Phased approach, however, is focused on iterative wins, piloting Agile within a group, then scaling it as you learn more over time.

Net Impact Curve

Phased approaches are relatively low-risk efforts while Big Bang approaches have a range of potential outcomes with varying levels of success.

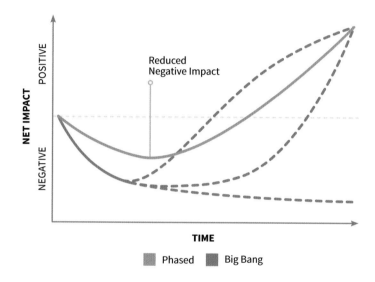

Source: Adapted from David Wilkinson, 2016[4]

In Chapter 8, the Phased approach, also called Nail and Scale, is explored in more depth. Anecdotally, the more popular and effective of the two is Phased. However, be flexible and adaptable in how you implement Agile. Sometimes market and corporate realities require dramatic and decisive action, so the Big Bang approach may be the optimal path. Still, there are clear risks and trade-offs with this approach. The sudden change can create a sense of insecurity or fear.[5] Remember, you're the leader, so it's your call; analyze, assess, and implement the right approach for your corporation.

Spotlight

Creating a Collective Vision

Laurie Nicoletti
Mastercard, VP of Product Development

Efficiency is the one word Laurie Nicoletti always comes back to when asked to describe Agile. It is one commonly forgone in an Agile transformation in favor of others like *transparency* and *collaboration*. But, Nicoletti, who has years of experience leading global business units as a Scaled Agile Transformation Leader and as Vice President at Mastercard, argues, "The underlying theme of Agile is to efficiently get products and solutions into the hands of the customer."

This is not to say, however, that the more people-centric outcomes of Agile are not as important. In fact, it is quite the opposite. Nicoletti notes that "having an aligned vision of Agile is one of the most powerful precursors to successful Agile in the workplace." In trying to achieve this Agile vision, Nicoletti and the Agile Development team at Mastercard focus on the team members involved.

In Nicoletti's experience with Agile transformation and project management, she has found that those who are not aligned with Agile, or who are detractors, often raise concerns because of a fear of the unknown. However, if this fear can be assuaged through respect and visibility of a common goal or vision, Nicoletti has seen that very few leaders or team members are likely to continue finding fault with Agile, or any other methodology for that matter.

Another measure Nicoletti and her team employ to ensure a collective vision is to take the time to recognize team members and their efforts. At Mastercard, "a significant chunk of quarterly Program Increment planning sessions is dedicated to appreciating what was done throughout that previous quarter and recognizing the efforts made by specific teams or individuals." Since the implementation of these small gestures, Nicoletti has found that team members have become much more comfortable with Agile in the organization, inculcating exponential traction as that element of fear and the unknown dissipates.

Retrospective
Agilesson 1: Initiate with Intent

START

- Instilling a collective vision of "Why Agile?" to help bring your team along on the journey

- Creating an environment that fosters the one-team mentality, one in which team members unite under an aligned goal

- Establishing mechanisms and processes to ensure collaboration among all team members, regardless of role or rank

- Empowering your team members by acting as a servant-leader throughout the transformation

- Setting realistic expectations to avoid disgruntled or disengaged team members

STOP / AVOID

- Ingraining the one-team mentality only by identifying good team members; also reinforce the mentality yourself

- Acting without understanding preexisting societal beliefs surrounding corporate executives

- Underestimating the time and effort required for an Agile transformation

- Using a Phased approach without considering other options that may work better for your unique circumstances

QUESTIONS

- How aligned is your corporate and Agile vision across the enterprise?

- How can you create a workplace where the best team players support, encourage, and work closely with others?

- What can you do as a leader to help create and nurture the one-team culture?

- How can you set expectations that are realistic for your team?

CHAPTER 6

Agilesson 2:

Cultivate Your Culture

Supportive business cultures are paramount to the success of an Agile transformation. As such, instill an environment of mutual trust, understand your unique geographic and cultural sensitivities, celebrate successes, and learn from failures.

Agile Begins with Your Change Champions

Find and leverage your transformation supporters.

When creating the one-team mentality, properly positioning your transformation supporters can pay immense dividends, often providing the impetus a corporation needs. Ashley Craft Fiore of Honeywell agrees, advising leaders: "Make sure that you're identifying your champions and positioning them strategically throughout the organization." This sentiment is further reinforced by the Agile Manifesto, which says "Build projects around motivated individuals," and by Everett Rogers' Adoption Curve, which explains that it's hard to convince a group of people of a controversial idea; instead, start with the minority that will champion it.[1]

Everett Rogers' Adoption Curve

Here start your transformation with your innovators and your early adopters – allow them to thrive and succeed to enhance the likelihood of success.

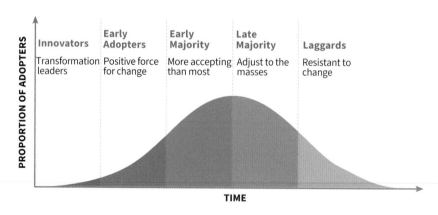

Source: Adapted from Value Based Management, Accessed 2020[2]

This is especially important in an Agile transformation, which requires significant momentum to implement successfully. If you can get the right people in the right roles, an Agile spark will more likely

Spotlight

A Special Type of Change Champion

Jennifer Morelli
Grant Thornton, Principal, Business Change Enablement

Jennifer Morelli, Principal at Grant Thornton, specializes in large-scale transformations and has nearly fifteen years of extensive experience strategizing, developing, and delivering organizational change management programs across numerous corporations and industries. Through these experiences, Morelli found that the largest challenge inherent to a transformation is the necessary shift of mindset and behavior. And while this shift "needs to happen to everyone across the corporation, within all ranks and roles," empowering executives and leaders to model and visibly support this shift can provide the impetus and momentum a transformation needs to succeed.

Unfortunately, in Agile transformations, it is often the corporate leaders who find the most difficulty in changing their mindsets. This is not a surprise as, often, leaders are in their role because they have historically found success in the traditional hierarchical structures. To help them along on their journey, Morelli suggests "sitting down and aligning on the benefits and outcomes of a transformation, but also the actions and changes necessary along the way."

Morelli stresses that some leaders will not be comfortable with the aforementioned necessary changes, especially the loss of control inherent to Agile, and that's okay. In these scenarios, Morelli suggests returning to her original advice: utilize the executives and leaders who are aligned to this new way of working to model the change they want to see and reinforce the personal, departmental, and organizational value.

The importance of this idea is emphasized by Morelli, as she believes it will help not only team members along on the journey, but other executives as well, as they are more able to draw on the similarities in the experiences they have and the changes they need to realize or accomplish. She has seen, first hand, that "when corporations are able to realize this level of alignment on the leadership level, they are far more likely to be successful with the overarching transformation."

meet the tinder, catch fire, and spread at an accelerated rate. This grass-roots adoption phenomenon should be recognized as a powerful tool in driving an Agile transformation and can be utilized by finding and leveraging your supporters.

> "Make sure that you're identifying your champions and positioning them strategically throughout the organization."
>
> **Ashley Craft Fiore**, *Honeywell*

Gathering the right people to be champions is not as simple as finding your best employees. Your champions could be diligent workers but not your high performers. Oddly, this is actually better for the transformation. Having champions who truly understand and support the cause, no matter what their previous performance within the organization, will have more influence than top performers who are doubtful. As these change champions advocate for agile, and peers start to buy into the process, success will likely begin to catch fire.

Having change champions not only will influence the success of your transformation, but also instill a culture that aligns both with current and future business needs. While corporations may not want to uproot their entire culture for a transformation, there, inevitably, will be cultural changes. These changes in culture will not happen overnight, and by having loyal transformation advocates – your change champions – there is the opportunity for cultural impact to account for the changing needs of the business while still maintaining the needs of employees. By having these champions spread across the organization, the diversity of perspectives and experiences at all levels are able to be heard.

After identifying and positioning your champions across the corporation, celebrate them to ensure continued success. For example, consider small gestures like peer recognition, a work-from-home opportunity, or even a day off after completing a milestone. Whatever you choose, it's imperative that the team knows that they're valued. As an added opportunity, you'll be able to share with others the factors that led to success.

Change Agent Traits

Leverage change agents to generate organizational buy-in and advance the vision of "why."

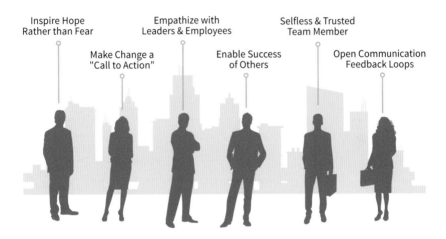

Inspire Hope
Rather than Fear

Empathize with
Leaders & Employees

Selfless & Trusted
Team Member

Make Change a
"Call to Action"

Enable Success
of Others

Open Communication
Feedback Loops

Source: Adapted from Value Based Management, Accessed 2020

Mutual Trust Is Key

Build and sustain trust through open communication and effective interactions.

Warren Buffett said, "It takes 20 years to build a reputation and five minutes to ruin it." A team's trust can be broken through poor behaviors or actions, like failure to recognize performance, overly critical attitudes, unrealistic expectations, micro-management, and many others. For the one-team model to be successful, it's imperative that leaders build on and sustain the trust and relationships they've established with their teams and leverage their change champions. As Marcus Johnson puts it succinctly, "For Agile to really work, you have to not only empower the teams, but also build and sustain mutual trust."

To engender trust, provide the "what" and "why," but leave the "how" to the teams. Agile leaders should spearhead transformations and bring everyone along on the journey, but give team members independence and autonomy. "We offer a lot more flexibility and a lot more experimentation," says Junius Rowland, IT Manager, Agile Delivery Office at AutoZone, "as long as the team is open and transparent about what they're doing and why." This is important in an Agile culture, as leaving the "how" to your teams allows them to find their own methods and solutions, accelerating innovative ideas to the forefront, not ones dictated or handed down.

Modes of Communication

Rely on personable communication methods to ensure effectiveness and clarity, and to build trust.

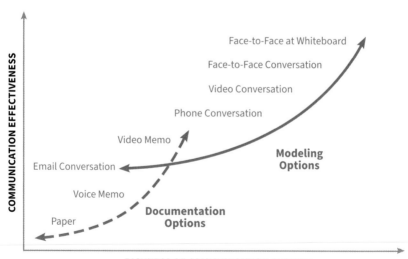

Source: Adapted from Scott Ambler and Alistair Cockburn, Accessed 2020[3]

Spotlight

Instill Trust to Find Success

David Fisher
North Highland, Principal

David Fisher, an accomplished and seasoned agilist with over twelve years of experience, is currently the Global Agile Change Management Lead at North Highland. In this role he delivers Agile, organizational effectiveness, and other change transformations for local and global multinational clients. Through these experiences, Fisher came to understand "while instilling effective communication is a pivotal step in transformations, Agile or otherwise, what is arguably more important is empowering the mutual trust that will underscore and drive the communication in the first place."

Fisher stresses that to build this trust, "leaders will need to break out of the traditional mindsets that have, historically, worked well for them, and, instead, embrace the unknown and unfamiliar Agile one." In this Agile mindset, leaders of a corporation provide the vision, the "why," but they leave the "how" to their teams.

Fisher further explains: "It's very similar to how Product Owners drive the prioritization and vision, but leave 'how to get it done' to the team members themselves. Where organizations go wrong, however, is that they confine this mindset to just Product Owners. Instead, it needs to be shared by all leadership across the organization."

To help leaders through this transition, Fisher first helps them understand their strengths and how those strengths can fit within Agile: "At the end of the day, leaders need to understand how they can adapt their role. Those who are in a position to set the product vision could transition to a product management role. Those who are skilled at clearing roadblocks for their teams can transition into a Chief Scrum Master–like role." Fisher has experienced first-hand how difficult this transition can be, but finds that the corporations that are able to do so are more likely to realize true mutual trust and Agile success.

Another way to engender trust is to create and maintain open lines of effective communication. To do this, common barriers to open communication, like high stress, conflicting body language, and lack of focus or clarity around goals, must be overcome. Many of these issues can be managed through the simple use of face-to-face communication, the preferred mode of communication by many Agile practitioners. To illustrate, the previous graph, by internationally recognized computer scientist and Agile Manifesto signatory Alistair Cockburn, shows how effective communication can improve Agile software development. As described through Media Richness theory, face-to-face interaction is the most effective communication channel in regard to its richness, defined as "the learning that can be pumped through the medium."

> "For Agile to really work, you have to not only empower the teams, but also build and sustain mutual trust."
>
> **Marcus Johnson**, *Highmark Health*

Like any transformation, building trust into an enterprise takes time and effort, but is well worth the investment. As the world moves toward an agility-focused way of working, this type of culture will become more necessary, but it's important to be open to all modes of communication channels, especially as the market changes. For example, the coronavirus disease (COVID-19) pandemic led companies to rely on remote co-location rather than face-to-face communication. Teams that work in an Agile manner still had to make strides on their Sprints, but had to approach communication differently. Through this trust from leadership, teams explored other avenues to communicate to ensure the work would still get done. Remember Warren Buffett's words of wisdom and maintain the trust you've already built across the team.

Spotlight

Building a Trusting Work Environment

Max Ekesi
Whole Foods Market, Agile Program Manager

From twelve years of experience leading Agile transformations for Fortune 500 corporations, Max Ekesi, Agile transformation lead for the Whole Foods Market IT eCommerce department, has found one thing to be abundantly clear: "In order to foster a successful large-scale Agile transformation initiative, it is essential that all individuals and teams are engaged, empowered, and motivated." This starts with having the right people, but leaders must also nurture the right environment to support them.

More specifically, Ekesi believes an environment built on trust will allow autonomy and freedom to proliferate, ensuring the engagement, empowerment, and motivation your teams need to succeed. To help nurture this environment, Ekesi stresses that "the first step should always be to make sure you have open lines of communication." In doing so, team members across the corporation, regardless of position or rank, are able to interact openly and freely, building mutual trust along the way.

Another way Ekesi helps ensure such an environment is to cultivate a people-centric culture. Ekesi has achieved this at Whole Foods Market, now a subsidiary of Amazon, by championing a number of measures or practices. He believes, however, that the most important was co-locating teams. He stresses that this is a "tried and true method of empowering teams to work together, accomplish their goals faster, and realize greater success." Another measure Ekesi suggests leaders do is to "listen to your people. When they know that their voice is heard and valued, they will give back, committing themselves to the success of the company."

Implementing these practices has made a huge impact on the teams at Whole Foods. Ekesi has seen not only productivity skyrocket, but the amount of engagement, communication, and positive interactions increase as well. This has cultivated an environment where individuals and teams trust one another, enabling a successful Agile journey.

Failure Is Fine

Accept failure and treat it as a steppingstone.
Learn from mistakes, improve, and evolve.

Tesla, PayPal, SpaceX, Neuralink – these world-class organizations have become household names. Often overlooked, however, are the failures they endured along the way. For example, whether it's the failed rockets, the near-bankruptcy of Tesla and SpaceX, or the production woes of the Model 3, Elon Musk has had his fair share of failures.[5] However, instead of shying away, he embraces them as a necessity on the path to success. As Musk puts it, "Failure is an option here. If things are not failing, you are not innovating enough."[6]

Tesla's Transformation

Tesla learned from its mistakes, corrected its issues, and increased deliveries by 216% in subsequent quarters.

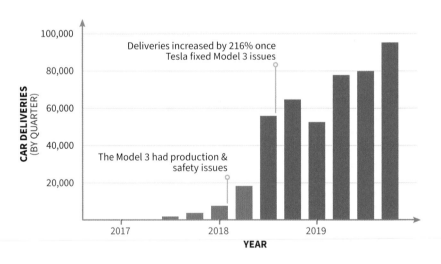

Source: Adapted from Zachary Shahan, 2020; Robert Ferris, 2017[7]

Embracing failure is just as important as recognizing successes. Maintaining this mindset is essential in any corporation that is considering implementing Agile. Termed "fail fast, fail often," it is the belief that

Spotlight

Accepting Failure

Phil Koserowski
The Leading Hotels of the World, VP, Marketing Executive

I f an organization looks to Agile as a means to drive innovation, one of the most important, and often most difficult, values that executives should embrace is the notion of "fail small, fail fast." At The Leading Hotels of the World (LHW), Phil Koserowski has done this by cultivating a culture where failure is not shied away from, but, instead, embraced as an opportunity to innovate.

To do this, he set aside a portion of a recurring team meeting dedicated to what is now called "Failure of the Month," an event where team members submit their "failures" and discuss them as a team. Koserowski notes that the practice, which promotes "the culture of trying something, failing and learning from it, and applying those learnings," wasn't easy at first. By publicly talking about these failures, however, Koserowski has helped create not only an organizational culture where failure is embraced, but an environment where team members can collectively celebrate and learn from them.

One such example involved a new component of their award-winning Loyalty Program, which had recently relaunched. This new program was well received by guests, but the internal build and execution of the new feature did not have a positive ROI. Instead of glossing over this fact, the team held a retrospective to review the results and assess what went wrong and why. These insights have resulted in key adjustments to the next planned activity that will drive a positive ROI.

Koserowski found that, ever since the inception of "Failure of the Month," teams all across The Leading Hotels of the World have become more transparent and collaborative as they work together toward a more agile and innovative organization. He urges other companies to consider similar concepts: "Do not avoid or overlook failures; instead, attack them head on."

failure can, and should, be celebrated through continual learning and refinement. "Fail fast, fail often" is a mantra among Agile practitioners and has brought much success to enterprises that have embraced it. Dave Witkin, Principal at Packaged Agile, warns us of the contrary approach: "Problems arise if you don't create an environment that allows failure."

To instill this mantra in your corporation, first help your teams understand why failure and learning from failure is critical, using examples like Elon Musk to support your viewpoint. But, also stress the following: "Fail, but fail smart." Each failure is a small win worth celebrating, but only if you evaluate and learn from them and apply those insights going forward. One of the principles of the Agile Manifesto underscores a complementary idea: "At regular intervals, the team reflects on how to be more effective, then tunes and adjusts its behavior accordingly."

> "Problems arise if you don't create an environment that allows failure."
>
> **Dave Witkin**, *Packaged Agile*

Following your team's understanding of "why," empower them to fail, with the appropriate guardrails, by incenting risk-taking with less regard to the outcome. Take, as an example, Phil Koserowski, marketing executive at The Leading Hotels of the World (LHW), who implemented a "Failure of the Month" award. This award was not a time to point fingers; rather, it was an opportunity to learn what failed, how it failed, and what the broader organization could learn from it. Many others at LHW, including their CEO and CFO, attributed Koserowski's style of continual learning as a key ingredient in the successful Agile transformation achieved at The Leading Hotels of the World.

You will encounter many roadblocks to embracing this mindset. One example could be the traditional corporate culture in which employees are conditioned to fear autonomy, risk-taking, and failure. As discussed, you need to be the one to champion this change and find other champions to support the cause. To do this, utilize the learnings from earlier in this chapter, and nurture an environment of mutual trust, transparency, and collaboration.

Another roadblock you might encounter is the time required to instill this mindset. Cultural changes will not happen overnight. As an executive, you need to understand this and you need to make sure your teams do as well. Be patient, keep your head up, and know that, with time, this effort will transform your enterprise into an organization of tomorrow.

Geographical Sensitivities and Considerations

Tailor your implementation approach to accommodate your corporation's cultural diversity.

Globalization has disrupted the workplace and will continue to do so. As such, corporations must force themselves to be flexible, accounting for different cultural backgrounds of their team members across the world. Just as an enterprise must adapt their unique culture to account for organizational changes, they must also account for the impact it may have on employees located in different countries, regions, or cities.

Take, for example, the need to adapt your communication style to convey a cohesive and unified vision. When considering a large geographic footprint, accounting for how employees around the world digest communication will enable you to communicate a more aligned vision. Understand that employees in different areas of the world may respond differently to the adoption of Agile as well. An Agile executive or coach who has only worked with teams in the Western Hemisphere should not expect identical approaches to be as successful in other parts of the world.

To illustrate, Agile coaches David Spinks and Glaudia Califano traveled the world to explore how geographical sensitivities impact Agile adoption. They found that cultural subtleties will impact how

Agile is perceived and adopted. For example, "[companies in] Argentina really embraced the Agile value of customer collaboration over contract negotiation. They were not afraid to come up with ideas [with customer insights]." Alternatively, "In the UK, there is a legacy of 'Tayloristic' management practices. To empower teams, this approach has to be unlearned for Agile to work as intended." Their experience reinforces how much geographical differences can impact the adoption of Agile.[8]

> "I was stunned by how similar we are. All the fundamentals of human spirit and behavior, respect, trust, embarrassment, it's all there. If you have people that understand this … Agile will work."
>
> **Crawfurd Hill**, *Encompass Corporation*

Others, however, believe that the need to account and strategize for these differences should be deprioritized. Instead, enterprises should focus on sustaining one inclusive business culture to nurture and accommodate all. That's because Agile is about having good people who understand how teams work. Crawfurd Hill, Corporate Agility Director at Encompass Corporation, says, "It's in the absence of this [culture] that you just get catastrophe." By building the right culture, it will enable teams to work past potential differences toward a common goal. Crawfurd Hill further underscores this sentiment through his experience leading transformations with people across seven different time zones and from more than fifty cultural backgrounds: "I was stunned by how similar we are. All the fundamentals of human spirit and behavior, respect, trust, embarrassment; it's all there. If you have people who understand this and the culture to empower them to do so, Agile will work."

Spotlight

Agile Across Culture and Geography

Steven HK Ma

No Moss Consulting, Chief Purpose Officer

Steven Ma, an international expert in agile organizational design, has advised numerous scaling organizations in their efforts to successfully bridge geography and culture. Ma advises that the values of each specific region (sometimes, regions within a nation) must be accounted for, adjusted to, supported, and included appropriately in order to design a successful Agile change approach.

For example, while working on several transformations in Australia, Ma found that the regional business culture, at the time, focused primarily on security and safety and avoided failure and risk. Obviously a barrier to Agile adoption, Ma, accordingly, placed extra focus on the benefits and outcomes of Agile to help his Australian clients overcome this fear of failure and risk. Ma has found that those in the United States and United Kingdom also have unique cultural values, citing that they "place great emphasis on innovation. This enables them to more easily adopt Agile as its benefits tie directly to what these organizations are prioritizing."

Besides cultural differences, a similar, but distinct aspect to account for when implementing Agile is the various government and leadership styles of a given region. In the Asian Tiger economies, government investment in education for modern approaches such as agility have enabled a younger workforce that is culturally and educationally more ready to be innovative and progressive. The emphasis placed on credentials means that Agile adoption should be tweaked to include significant formal training and certification programs. Another example: In the Middle East, it is government-led reforms that have enabled private and family firms to be encouraged to be more innovative and entrepreneurial in attempting to establish angel investment groups.

As Ma continues to advise corporations around the world, he believes he will continue to find these adoption nuances that can affect anyone on their Agile journey, for better or worse. He encourages executives to do the same as corporations continue to grow and reach far differing geographies, and the cultures and values within.

Cultural Considerations

Consider cultural influences when deploying Agile globally to increase the effectiveness of adoption.

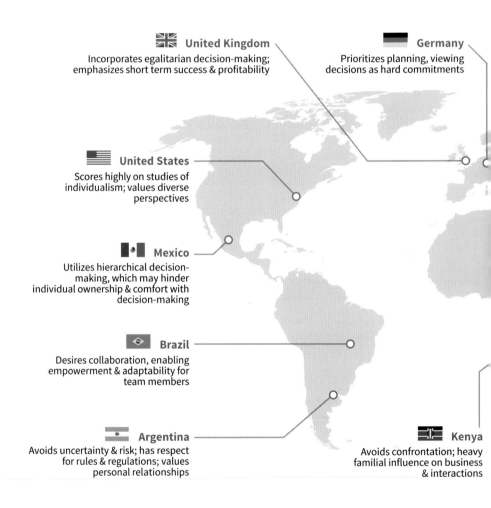

United Kingdom
Incorporates egalitarian decision-making; emphasizes short term success & profitability

Germany
Prioritizes planning, viewing decisions as hard commitments

United States
Scores highly on studies of individualism; values diverse perspectives

Mexico
Utilizes hierarchical decision-making, which may hinder individual ownership & comfort with decision-making

Brazil
Desires collaboration, enabling empowerment & adaptability for team members

Argentina
Avoids uncertainty & risk; has respect for rules & regulations; values personal relationships

Kenya
Avoids confrontation; heavy familial influence on business & interactions

Source: Composite of DayBlink, 2020[9]

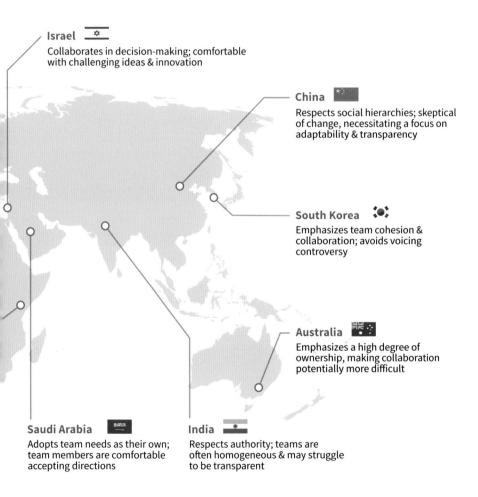

Israel
Collaborates in decision-making; comfortable with challenging ideas & innovation

China
Respects social hierarchies; skeptical of change, necessitating a focus on adaptability & transparency

South Korea
Emphasizes team cohesion & collaboration; avoids voicing controversy

Australia
Emphasizes a high degree of ownership, making collaboration potentially more difficult

Saudi Arabia
Adopts team needs as their own; team members are comfortable accepting directions

India
Respects authority; teams are often homogeneous & may struggle to be transparent

Retrospective
Agilesson 2: Cultivate Your Culture

START

- Identifying and strategically placing your change champions across the corporation to create transformation momentum

- Celebrating team members across the organization to ensure they understand that they are valued

- Providing the "what" and "why," but trusting your team with the "how" to accelerate innovative ideas to the forefront

- Embracing failure on your path to corporate agility by using each failure as a learning opportunity

- Accounting for geographical and cultural considerations when deploying Agile

STOP / AVOID

- Prescribing predefined solutions as the only means to succeed; this often stifles adaptability and innovation

- Looking only to your high performers when identifying change champions; instead, find those who truly support the transformation

- Failing without failing smart; remember, failures are only worth celebrating if you evaluate and learn from them

- Expecting Agile to be uniformly adopted or accepted in the various backgrounds and cultures that make up your corporation

QUESTIONS

- How will you identify who your change champions are and where they should be positioned?

- Do your team members embrace failure and, if not, how can you help them do so?

- What are the various communication channels that you can establish to help instill mutual trust?

- How will you identify the various backgrounds and cultures you work with and, conseuquently, adjust your transformation approach?

Agilesson 3:

Transform Your Team

Employees are the heart of your business; understanding, accommodating, and leveraging their diversity is paramount. On your path toward corporate agility, ensure that this diversity in learning, working, and growing is accounted for.

Invest in Your Most Important Resource – Your People

Leverage your Human Resources (HR) department and minimize your reliance on third-party organizations.

You and your organization know and understand your customers, competitors, limitations, and opportunities better than anyone else. It is common and prudent for corporations to seek outside counsel to help guide them through uncharted waters. That said, in implementing Agile, think twice before bringing in third parties to manage the entire transformation; instead, leverage internal resources, early and wherever possible, and grow the team from within. Art Moore of Clear Systems further underscores this sentiment when he says, "The stumble happens when organizations bring in consultants under the mistaken belief that others can make the organization lean and agile on their behalf. After all, it is only those in the organization who can create agility."

> "The stumble happens when organizations bring in consultants under the mistaken belief that others can make the organization lean and agile on their behalf. After all, it is only those in the organization who can create agility."
>
> **Art Moore**, *Clear Systems LLC*

This is not to say that external advisors are not valuable. If needed, consider bringing in small teams to strategize, advise, and augment your teams and instill process discipline. Understand, though, that to be agile and achieve lasting corporate agility, you require the right people. Hiring decisions based primarily on certifications can, and likely will, lead to failed implementations. Rather, bring in those who have real experience driving real transformations. Junius Rowland, IT Manager, Agile

Delivery Office at AutoZone, emphasizes this point when he says, "A lot of allegedly 'qualified people' don't understand the 'why' of corporate agility. Successful leaders seek out those who do."

Agile Certification Snapshot

At the time of publication, the perceived value of various Agile certifications does not align with the level of experience required to obtain said certifications.

	Certification Body	Cost (USD)	Work Experience Prerequisites	Education Prerequisites	Difficulty to Obtain
Certified ScrumMaster (CSM)	ScrumAlliance	~ $595	None	None	Low
Agile Certified Practitioner (ACP)	Project Management Institute	~ $495	12-Months of Agile Experience	4-Year University	Medium
SAFe Consultant (SPC)	Scaled Agile	~ $799	None	None	Low
Agile Certified Coach (ACC)	ICAgile	~ $1,795	None	None	Low
Adv. Certified ScrumMaster (A-CSM)	ScrumAlliance	~ $1,295	12-Months of Agile Experience	None	Medium

Source: Composite of DayBlink, 2020[i]

"A lot of allegedly 'qualified people' don't understand the 'why' of corporate agility. Successful leaders seek out those who do."

Junius Rowland, *AutoZone*

Leverage internal resources and focus on insourcing through HR and your recruiting process. Agile is not for everyone so it's important to find and develop those who are more likely to be successful. For example, a candidate who has lived through a failed transformation in the past could find it difficult getting behind another one. Or, the Agile value "responding to change over following a plan" may not resonate with some employees' working style. HR must be cognizant of the behaviors and traits that will and will not fit in an Agile environment. By understanding these behaviors and traits, HR should be able to identify and attract individuals who will thrive within your new ways of working.

> "This Agile journey is something that I was clearly invested in and so I wanted to make sure that I had the right people that had the capacity, attitude, and skill set."
>
> **Phil Koserowski**, *The Leading Hotels of the World*

HR should also adjust performance assessments to identify top-performing agilists within the company, prioritizing metrics that Agile inherently values such as collaboration, innovation, and continuous improvement over other more traditional metrics. Reprioritizing and fine-tuning these metrics allows you to celebrate those who are driving toward corporate agility.

For a transformation to be successful, Agile or otherwise, ensure you have the right people to get it done. As Phil Koserowski of The Leading Hotels of the World says, "This journey is something that I was clearly invested in, so I wanted to make sure that I had the right people that had the capacity, attitude and skill set." Once you have the right people, however, don't let them go! Too often do corporations go out of their way to hand-pick their teams, then let those teams dissipate. Yes, situations will arise. But, as best you can, keep your people together.

Spotlight

Certificates, Experience, and Evolution

Sondra Ashmore, Ph.D

Berkley Technology Services LLC, AVP and Business Partner

Sondra Ashmore is an experienced business leader with expertise in leveraging technology to optimize business performance. Through these experiences, she has garnered special distinctions as a "Forty under 40" business leader and a recipient of the Iowa Technology Association's Women of Innovation award. She attributes most of her success not to her extensive classroom training, but rather to her constant learning and growth in the field.

Throughout her career Ashmore has observed popular Agile certifications, such as "Certified ScrumMaster" or "Certified Product Owner," to be attractive certifications for practitioners because they can be completed in a matter of days and do not have recertification requirements. Additionally, there are some certification programs that require ongoing training and experience, such as the Project Management Institute's Agile Certified Practitioner (PMI-ACP), and these are the certifications Ashmore encourages people to maintain. Since initially receiving the PMI-ACP certification in 2011, she has benefited from the continual training required to maintain the certification. She goes on to say "Certifications, similar to Agile, should change and evolve, and people should seek to recertify and continue their Agile education."

Ashmore stresses that all certification courses are helpful, as they are an effective way to introduce the basics of an Agile way of working. However, this, alongside other Agile training, should only be considered as a starting point. Without real-world experience and building upon the training one receives, that training will become less useful and relevant over time. Ashmore believes that the ever-evolving nature of Agile will only work to bolster this phenomenon: as Agile inevitably changes, so, too, will the certifications that cover it.

To adapt, Ashmore suggests implementing training specialized to your corporation. This can help practitioners within your corporation keep up to date on the particulars and nuances of your unique Agile approach. Still, Ashmore stresses her original lesson: "Certifications can be a great starting point to your Agile journey; ensure, however, that you are continuously learning along the way."

Develop Your Agile Competency

Arm the right people using the right Learning
and Development (L&D) programs.

Once you've identified the right team members, provide them with the resources to support their L&D. To ensure this is done correctly, your L&D program should begin with a small group, gathering their feedback and refining the program as needed, and then scaling and continuously evolving along the way.

Introducing a new methodology can be complicated, so ensure that your L&D program is easy to execute and maintains a clear message. As General Electric's Jack Welch stated, "Simplicity is the essence of managing people. You've got to be simple and consistent to get everybody on the same page." However, at the same time, successful leaders must demonstrate a comprehensive understanding of the transformation process, including insight into how it will impact each participant, both now and in the future.

Building Corporate Agility
Rapidly build a corporate Agile capability: strategize, start small, then scale.

1	2	3	4
Select Change Methodology	**Develop Training Strategy**	**Pilot Training Program**	**Roll Out Enterprise Program**
• Define Business Needs	• Communicate & Align	• Execute Program	• Iterate *(as needed)*
• Gain Leadership Buy-in	• Simplify & Start Small	• Assess & Refine	• Roll Out Strategically
• Craft Unique Solution	• Gamify *(if possible)*	• Choose Pilot Group	• Customize Program

Source: DayBlink, 2020

Spotlight

Using L&D Programs to Help in the Transformation

Christen McLemore
HeyMac Consulting LLC, Founder

With decades of experience coaching and leading Agile transformations at leading corporations like GE Transportation, Mastercard, AOL, among others, Christen McLemore decided to create her own company, which parleys her earlier roles and consults Fortune 100 corporations on their Agile journey. Through these experiences, she identified many common challenges that corporations face. One of the most important is ensuring that the existing Learning & Development (L&D) curriculum is appropriately adjusted as Agile begins disseminating across a corporation.

The first L&D adjustment McLemore stresses corporations must make is ensuring the proper training for the different team members involved. As a trainer herself, she understands that "many of these classes that companies send employees off to are mostly about just the framework. They aren't nearly as effective at teaching how someone, especially a leader, fits in the whole process."

As a result, she maintains that the corporations that employ third parties to drive the transformation should first consider how the proposed framework will be embedded with the existing L&D and HR curriculums and processes, and ensure all team members have specialized education on their role in Agile. When corporations fail to do this, she finds many team members, especially middle and senior management, fail to make the adjustments they need to be successful.

McLemore cites this failure of management as the reason she transitioned into an advisory role in the first place: "I felt the need to step in because I saw the human side, particularly at the middle and senior management level, being neglected, precisely where many transformations start to go wrong." Her urge to step in was further bolstered as many leaders didn't realize that their actions were sabotaging the transformation. McLemore has seen, however, that once these different roles are uniquely addressed, the transformation is in a much better position to succeed.

To achieve this, leading corporations customize training for different segments. For example, the L&D program for an executive sponsor may focus on enacting change and identifying value streams while that for staff may relate more to day-to-day processes. Too often, corporations use off-the-shelf educational programs that are not designed for specific teams and their work. Avoid this by understanding the specific L&D needs of your people, and what would benefit them the most. Your path to corporate agility is unique, so be sure to carry that message into all facets of the process, including your L&D programs. Marcus Johnson discovered this firsthand at Highmark Health: "Every Agile transformation requires extremely different ways of educating, digesting, and implementing. Customize and simplify for each."

> "Every Agile transformation requires extremely different ways of educating, digesting, and implementing. Customize and simplify for each."
>
> **Marcus Johnson**, *Highmark Health*

Knowing your team and how they will respond to L&D programs is critical for transformational success. A unique approach that many executives have found effective is the gamification of education sessions and interactive workshops. For example, Sondra Ashmore of Berkley Technology Services LLC suggests "education should be offered in environments that are less day-to-day working conditions, but more akin to hackathons or Code Jam sessions." Of course, not all executives will prefer this method of learning and some might opt instead for a traditional classroom setting, which can also be quite effective. It's all about finding the approach that works best for you and your corporation.

> "Education should be offered in environments that are less day-to-day working conditions, but more akin to hackathons or Code Jam sessions."
>
> **Sondra Ashmore**, *Berkley Technology Services LLC*

There Will Be Detractors

The path to corporate agility is not for everyone. Identify your detractors and find ways to support them.

As with any workforce, your Agile teams will have their share of high and low performers. While some performance distributions may skew left or right, most of them can be characterized by a symmetrical bell curve or a normal distribution, seen in the graphic below. The pre-Agile and post-Agile performance distributions can be similar, but that is not always the case. Higher performers pre-Agile can continue their high performance within an Agile environment, but there will be instances where they won't. The same will hold true for lower performers as well.

Detractor Distribution Curve

Transformation detractors will largely consist of laggards and lower performers, but don't be surprised if some higher performers are detractors as well.

Source: DayBlink, 2020

Types of Detractors

Saboteurs pose the greatest threat to the success of an Agile transformation.

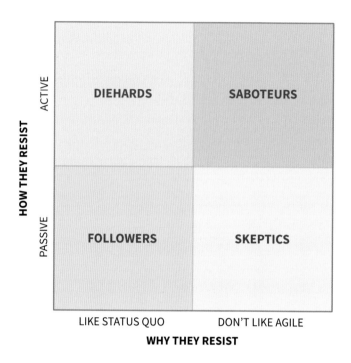

Source: Adapted from Mike Cohn, 2009⁴

Although detractors, those who row against your corporate agility efforts, can materialize on either end of the performance distribution, data suggests most tend to manifest in the low-performer ranks; as with all large populations, however, there will be outliers: a high-performing middle manager can become your biggest detractor because of changing roles (discussed later in the chapter). This phenomenon occurs regularly, not just because low performers perform below the median, or vice versa, but because low performers feel as if they won't be heard or understood in this new way of working.[3] As Max Ekesi of Whole Foods Market explains, "The biggest detractors often come from people's inability to, or fear of, change." To combat this, support all employees involved in your agile journey, regardless of their prior individual performance.

"Bringing everyone along on the journey" is a useful adage. However, to achieve corporate agility, corporations should seek to identify and address the underlying causes of the detraction. As shown previously, there are four categories of detractors. Understanding which of the four quadrants a detractor falls in will help you determine how to work effectively with them and, potentially, turn them into a supporter. That said, we understand that generalizing and placing individuals in "boxes" comes with inherent risks and should not be your only guide for finding ways to work with detractors. With this in mind, below are common characteristics that can be found within the four quadrants.

"Followers" are the first, and probably least disruptive, category. They embrace the status quo and traditional ways of working. They won't do much to undermine your corporate agility efforts, but you will need to emphasize that Agile will become the new status quo to gain buy-in from this segment.

"Skeptics" are the second category of detractors. They are a little more pernicious; they fundamentally do not share the values and principles of the Agile Manifesto. They are likely to indulge in passive-aggressive behavior, patterns that can do much to create organizational noise. To effectively engage with these detractors, align with them on basic agile etiquette, like attending meetings, following good agile practices, and using proper agile terminology.

"Diehards" are the third category of detractors. They love their current situation, be it the activities they do, the prestige they have, or the co-workers they work with. They don't necessarily oppose Agile values and principles; rather, they flout anything that undermines what they already have. This behavior can prove dangerous, as these individuals often try to convince those who are more likely to adopt Agile to "jump ship" and also become detractors.

"Saboteurs" are the final, and often most hazardous, category of detractors. They do not subscribe to Agile values and principles and actively hinder Agile from taking root and blossoming. Though the effort can be high, you can successfully engage these individuals and understand, on a case-by-case basis, the "why" underlying their counterproductive behavior. The good news is that proactive and consistent engagement can turn them around and make them strong supporters for Agile.

> "The biggest detractors often come from people's inability to, or fear of, change."
>
> **Max Ekesi**, *Whole Foods Market*

Know that all transformations come with resistance and friction. If you are not identifying and quelling the underlying causes of detractions, you will see the negative effects reflected in metrics like the Net Promoter Score (NPS) framework, which will be explored in later chapters.[4] While finding ways to support and work effectively with detractors to bring them around is the best way forward, there are other, last-resort ways to address the challenges posed by detractors. These include transitioning them to another team, shifting them to another part of the corporation that is outside the scope of the transformation, or helping them find new career opportunities outside the corporation.

To summarize, make gradual changes to gain buy-in along the way. Support and nudge those who need it, but don't try to do so overnight. Detractors will always exist but, oftentimes, they can be overcome by understanding the detractor characteristics and their underlying causes. As Laurie Nicoletti of Mastercard explains, "With detractors, you need to first understand if this is a miss with Agile, or something else? If we can break down their concerns, we can get to the root of the problem and solve it."

Spotlight

Helping Agile Detractors

Vamsi Tirnati
DXC Technology, CTO of Transportation

A gile is a different way of working and, as such, will inherently have many team members within an organization who will work against its adoption. In Vamsi Tirnati's twenty-two years of experience defining digital strategy for Fortune 100 corporations, he has found that the best way to mitigate the impact of these detractors and bring them along on the journey is by "doing the upfront preparation to craft a well-thought-out, tactical approach."

The first step of Tirnati's approach is to have company leaders discuss and align on "Where in the corporation?" To do this, he has leaders think about the different teams and departments within a corporation and the characteristics of each. Oftentimes, Tirnati finds that it is much easier to implement Agile within a group that is already predisposed to such a transformation. This group is typically composed of "individuals who are willing to remain flexible and open to change."

Once Agile is successfully implemented within this group, it can then be scaled to the rest of the organization. Tirnati understands that detractors are unavoidable, and often doubt the actual feasibility and benefits that are associated with Agile, but if they see a "Proof of Concept" of Agile successfully working within the corporation, it will do much to help them see how Agile can change day-to-day work for the better.

After the "where," Tirnati encourages leaders to also ask themselves "what" and "how." Those who practice Agile do a great job preaching its potential benefits, but these benefits are oftentimes not directly tied to a corporation's unique goals and objectives. Tirnati believes an implementation plan, specific to the corporation in question, "can help detractors understand what actual benefits can be realized for the corporation and how to realize them."

Evolve the Role of Middle Management

Understand that future leaders' expectations will change as many traditional upward mobility paths are upended in Agile transformations.

As discussed in earlier chapters, Agile decentralizes authority in the corporation and, therefore, impacts the traditional role of middle managers by affecting their locus of control, and doing away with roles once considered necessary. Traditional middle-manager responsibilities, such as assigning tasks, planning projects, documenting progress, and evaluating employees, will be subsumed by other responsibilities that come with the Agile journey. The potential fear and discontentment among middle managers that will likely result from Agile must be acknowledged and addressed in order to overcome their resistance, minimize churn in their ranks, and leverage their unique institutional knowledge and experience.

According to McKinsey & Company, supporting middle managers as they navigate through an Agile transformation can be well worth a corporation's time and effort: "Since many mid-level managers possess a wealth of experience, knowledge, and skill, redeploying them as hands-on individual contributors is one way to let them accomplish more than they do in managerial roles."[5] Another approach McKinsey & Company recommends is to give middle managers the training they need to move up to more senior leadership roles. You can support middle managers' transition by asking them to help teams succeed by providing inspiration, support and requisite resources.[6]

As corporate agility takes root, the ranks of middle managers will contract, thus "flattening" the organization. The traditional vertical model becomes more horizontal, reducing hierarchy levels, removing superfluous communication touchpoints, and, most importantly, migrating to a team-based structure. This new structure serendipitously serves to counter the Peter Principle: the concept that companies promote people until they reach a competency ceiling and therefore can't go any higher, but are also suboptimally leveraged within the organization.[7] By virtue of having fewer levels, a flattened structure inherently has fewer employees in positions they are not suited for and, conversely, more employees in positions they can thrive in.

Though corporations will not flatten completely, successful enterprises will get narrower, specifically at the middle management level. It's important to note that middle management will not disappear overnight, but certain roles and responsibilities will be reshaped and others will become obsolete. While managers will still need to manage up and strategize, they will manage down less frequently, and can, instead, focus on driving business value. For instance, some corporations see managers transition from a historical 50/50 people management/ strategy management ratio to something closer to 25/75.

Proactive executives provide opportunities for middle management to create value in this new environment. Consider this insight from Steve Elliott, who has worked with various middle managers through Agile transformations: "Probably the most consequential thing I do is to ensure everybody understands their role and how it fits within the bigger picture."

Debate exists across Agile leaders on how best to redeploy traditional managers. Some suggest they transition to a Product Owner (PO) role, a critical role within some Agile frameworks that contributes significant value to the business. For transformations that have a PO, such as Scrum, the PO has ownership of the product backlog, which includes all the tasks the team needs to work on to release or launch their product or offering. Additionally, POs need to actively manage the backlog to ensure that it is accurately prioritized and refined. However, other agilists disagree and take the position that managers shouldn't become POs due to potential reporting conflicts.

Regardless of your opinion on the future of this important population, most Fortune 500 executives agree it is important to win over the support of middle managers early on, and sometimes before the transformation begins. This can result in a higher degree of success as it has the potential to create fewer middle-manager detractors. Additionally, by engaging managers early on in the process they can identify their own path within the business. Although executives might be hesitant to share their decision-making authority with managers, remember most managers mastered those roles before moving into their current positions. Phil Koserowski said it best when describing how he shared responsibility with his management team: "It was a little uncomfortable to step back from some of the planning, but the team quickly demonstrated their ability to be self-directed."

> "It just means some managers are not going to have the same role and the same way of defining themselves and how they contribute to the organization. They're going to have to reevaluate."
>
> **Linda Rising,** *Independent Consultant*

It is important to remember that being agile is about prioritizing people. It's all about people. Therefore, it is imperative to leverage the strengths of middle managers in the pursuit of corporate agility, not seek to quickly eliminate them from payroll. As Linda Rising explains, "It just means some managers are not going to have the same role and the same way of defining themselves and how they contribute to the organization. They're going to have to reevaluate."

Spotlight

Evolving Middle Managers' Agile Roles

Ashley Craft Fiore
Honeywell, Director, Agile Program Management

Throughout her career and experience as an Agile executive, Ashley Craft Fiore found that executives implementing Agile need to be keenly aware of the role of middle managers and how it evolves during an Agile transformation. If leaders fail to take this evolution into account, Craft Fiore finds "middle managers can often become detractors as they find it difficult to understand how they fit within the Agile framework."

To mitigate this, Craft Fiore stressed that corporations must empower managers to transform out of the traditional role of "defending their kingdom," and into one where they can, instead, focus on nurturing and enabling their teams. In this new role, managers will be able to help their team members grow in the midst of an unknown Agile setting. Craft Fiore stresses that the value of helping managers transition to this new role cannot be understated as "it can greatly streamline and strengthen the overall process, and provide the momentum an Agile transformation needs to succeed."

Similarly, unsuccessful Agile transformations often feature managers who do not fully understand their new role, with many, instead, asserting themselves in leadership roles like Release Train Engineers, Product Owners, Scrum Masters, and others. While some have found success with this structure, Craft Fiore emphasizes that this narrow focus is often detrimental to an Agile transformation, as "team members who directly report to these types of managers do not always feel as if they can voice their concerns and failures."

This situation reestablishes a hierarchy that is in complete contradiction to the flatter organization Agile is trying to drive and will often lead to a suboptimal Agile implementation. To avoid this result, Craft Fiore stresses that executives work closely with middle managers throughout an Agile transformation, ensuring they are brought along on the journey.

Retrospective

Agilesson 3: Transform Your Team

START

- Leveraging HR to find and develop internal and external personnel likely to find success with Agile

- Adjusting performance standards to identify top-performing agilists within the corporation by prioritizing metrics that Agile inherently values

- Developing an adaptive and customizable L&D program for different roles within a corporation

- Bringing detractors along the journey by identifying and understanding the underlying causes of each detractor

- Helping middle managers transition to their new role early on, sometimes even before a transformation begins

STOP / AVOID

- Over-indexing on third-party help; if necessary, bring in small external teams with experience, not solely certifications

- Utilizing a single static L&D program, or one that is off-the-shelf, across the corporation

- Deprioritizing middle managers in the transformation process; it is imperative to leverage their strengths early and often

QUESTIONS

- How will you utilize HR to attract, retrain, and develop those who are likely to succeed in your Agile environment?

- How are your L&D programs developed and how can you improve the process?

- How will you identify your detractors and, consequently, help them along on the journey?

- How will you help your middle managers transition to this new, unfamiliar role?

CHAPTER 8

Agilesson 4:

Work Wisely

Simplicity is at the center of corporate agility. Focus on getting to the right solution, and then expand it across the corporation. To ensure further success, account for customers' needs at all stages of the journey.

Keep It Light

Simplify processes and minimize documentation to
help Agile flourish.

As teams across your corporation embark on the transformation journey, they will have to start working with corporate agility in mind. And the best way to start is to think simple. The tenth principle of the Agile Manifesto reads, "Simplicity – the art of maximizing the amount of work not done – is essential." To start this process, leaders should begin emphasizing efficiency in a way that limits unnecessary work. While challenging in concept, evidence from Fortune 500 executives suggests it can be highly advantageous if done correctly.

Take communication as an example. Corporate agility requires working autonomously, collaborating interactively, and promoting direct meetings with one another to create value. In contrast to this, traditional hierarchy forces this information to traverse up and down the chain of command, a less efficient and effective way of working. Teams focusing on prototyping and gathering fast customer feedback provide another example. They get working products out to the customer promptly and quickly pivot to incorporate feedback as needed, reducing the unnecessary rework often seen in traditional models.

In addition to streamlining processes, successful corporations simplify their documentation overhead. Burdensome and heavy documentation is a pain point that is mandated under many traditional ways of working. Agile processes and mindsets lessen the need for such documentation. Scott Ambler, co-founder of Disciplined Agile, recommends:[1]

- **Keep documentation just simple enough, but not too simple**: Comprehensive documentation does not translate necessarily to project success; in fact, it can increase your chance of failure.
- **Write the fewest documents with least overlap**: Overlapping documentation creates waste; rolling up smaller

documents into larger ones allows easier identification of areas of overlap.

- **Place the information in the appropriate place**: Keep documents in the appropriate location to minimize rework; also, consider pain points like indexing, linking, and accessibility for this.
- **Display information publicly**: The more straightforward and available your information, the less detailed your documentation needs to be.

Although considering the above is beneficial, remember to use the appropriate technology to short-cut your way to streamlined processes and simplified documentation. As discussed earlier in Chapter 1, leading corporations leverage tools like artificial intelligence, automation, or big data to cut down on administrative overhead. Beware, however, that these technologies, like Agile, require upfront time and effort to implement successfully, and often come with hidden costs.

Nail and Scale

Start small and scale iteratively, learning along the way.

As mentioned in Chapter 5, the Nail and Scale approach to implementing Agile can be effective. First popularized by Nathan R. Furr and Paul Ahlstrom in their book, *Nail It Then Scale It*, the approach encourages enterprises to start small with a pilot group, then scale iteratively to the rest of the organization, learning from successes and failures along the way.

Although this approach was introduced for entrepreneurs and Lean workstreams, it has found significant success within Agile. In fact, the data shows that using a Nail and Scale approach can reduce the amount of negative impact and reduce the time to realization of benefits when compared to the more traditional Big Bang approach. Jeff Sutherland,

Spotlight

Providing Clear Guardrails

Colin Ferguson
North Highland, Agile Transformation Principal

With over eighteen years of audit, traditional, and Agile project experience, Colin Ferguson has helped lead transformations while working at firms like North Highland and Duke Energy Corporation. Over the past ten years, as an Agile leader, Ferguson has found that focusing on a true Agile mindset and servant leadership mentality first will lead to better adoption of agile ways of working and can improve an agile transformation's sustainability overall. Ferguson explains further: "While defining consistent ways of working can drive efficiencies, it's important to encourage and develop the right culture to enable the efficiencies in the first place."

Ferguson stresses that it is often leadership who plays a critical role in developing this culture as they are responsible for communicating the strategy, providing context around the strategy, and implementing a clear governance model for the teams to operate within. To help corporations do this, Ferguson coaches executives to "provide clear guide rails and expectations around what's critical but empower and encourage teams to make autonomous decisions around the rest."

To help illustrate, Ferguson provides an analogy of federal and state laws: "If you're in the United States, the federal government mandates that all people drive on the right-hand side of the road, and mandates that the states enforce this. However, because the driving conditions are different state by state, they empower the states to set the speed limits themselves. Similarly, Ferguson finds that leaders who are comfortable with setting parameters and allowing their teams to operate autonomously within them find that the teams deliver better results because they are able to come up with creative ways to address each unique situation.

Agile Manifesto signatory and co-creator of Scrum, says it best: "We typically start small and we get something really working, get some good success … then we expand it."[2]

Phased and Big Bang Approaches

The Phased approach is a concentrated change effort while the Big Bang approach emphasizes a faster track to scale.

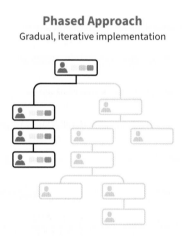

Phased Approach
Gradual, iterative implementation

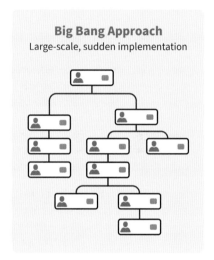

Big Bang Approach
Large-scale, sudden implementation

Source: DayBlink, 2020

The first step for a successful Nail and Scale approach is to choose a group or team for your initial Agile pilot. Vamsi Tirnati, CTO of Transportation at DXC Technology, points out, "There is always a leading-edge group, typically composed of individuals who are fast to change, flexible, and adaptable. Collaborating with these groups and starting off with smaller value streams is where I have seen a lot of success."

Don't overlook the work involved in this step, as it can and will likely be the catalyst for the momentum required to carry your transformation forward. Crawfurd Hill echoes this sentiment: "Use them to build the proof point, because it's in this proof point that Agile can work." Careful execution within the pilot team, early results, and demonstrated value will propagate excitement throughout the corporation. This concept is further underscored by Susan Marricone, Agility Transformation Leader at Honeywell, who stated, "Get a logical person in there doing something in an Agile way. Then, other teams will look at you and your terrific results. They'll look at your engaged and happy team and say, 'I want to do what they're doing.'"

> "There is always a leading-edge group, typically composed of individuals who are fast to change, flexible, and adaptable. Collaborating with these groups and starting off with smaller value streams is where I have seen a lot of success."
>
> **Vamsi Tirnati**, *DXC Technology*

Scaling of Agile
Find success in a pilot group, then scale your learnings across the corporation.

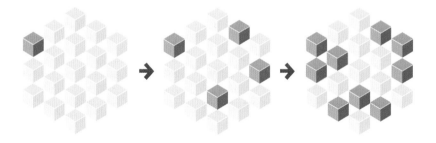

Source: DayBlink, 2020

Once you've established your pilot group and achieved some success, begin scaling to the rest of the organization. However, be aware of some common pitfalls, the main one being a lack of patience. Often, organizations will jump the gun and begin scaling before truly understanding what happened with the pilot team and how to best apply those lessons. Remember, the point of this method is to learn iteratively. If you are not doing so, you risk the worst of both worlds – all

Spotlight

The Nail and Scale Approach

Dr. Steve Mayner
Scaled Agile, Inc., SAFe Fellow & Principal Consultant

History suggests transformations require tailored approaches. However, there are still common patterns corporations follow to increase the likelihood of success. In his thirty-plus years of experience delivering innovative technology solutions and as a thought leader, coach, trainer, and consultant for Fortune 500 executives, Dr. Steve Mayner identified one of the more important patterns to utilize in a large-scale transformation: "Identify an area that is ripe for adoption and test change within that small pilot group. Then, slowly and iteratively scale that change to the rest of the corporation."

Dr. Mayner believes this plan of attack becomes even more important in the context of Agile. He helps executives employ it by providing a diagnostic model to identify potential candidate areas or groups with the largest opportunities. Some of the inputs used in this model include "the amount of working alignment between the leadership and team and the level of clarity and vision of the product."

To ensure this Nail and Scale approach is successful, Dr. Mayner emphasizes the importance of collecting fast feedback. This information can be leveraged to gauge whether working in an Agile manner is ideal for the particular environment, culture, and industry in question, and if not, whether there is anything that can be done to change those aspects to better fit an Agile approach. Furthermore, it enables teams to understand any mistakes that may have been made, learn from them, and apply those lessons in future endeavors.

Dr. Mayner believes the usefulness of a Nail and Scale approach is further underscored by the notion that "trends are always emerging and evolving, not only in the consumer marketplace, but also within Agile and other methodologies as well." Starting with a smaller group and then scaling provides the opportunity to pivot with these changes, enabling a more successful Agile transformation and superior business results.

the consequences of a Big Bang approach, namely a proliferation of fear, uncertainty, and lack of guidance, without its benefits.

Ideally, the scaling of Agile will happen naturally as more people gain exposure and an internal desire to use Agile. This doesn't mean, however, that you can't go out of your way to garner support. It is your job to inspire. In fact, many executives use internal marketing campaigns or other communication methods so that other teams are aware that Agile is being utilized. Then, those who are interested will naturally become involved and begin to learn about Agile.

Another way to scale is to establish metrics to continuously monitor and track improvements. The right metrics allow you to see if your actions are resulting in measurable improvements. These results can then be shared throughout the corporation, inspiring others to be agile and do Agile. However, as will be discussed in Chapter 9, ensure that you are using the right metrics; as with many things Agile, you will need time, effort, and many iterations to find them.

Focus on the Customer

Embed the customers' perspective into every
Agile team.

To thrive under Agile, your teams need to embrace customers and their needs. This is because a large portion of Agile, as underscored in the Agile Manifesto, is premised around "satisfying the customer through early and continuous delivery of valuable software." David Fisher, Principal at North Highland, echoes this sentiment, stating, "If it doesn't deliver value to the customer early and continuously, then it's not Agile." Ensure your team understands this. If they don't, it can and will likely bottleneck your transformation.

Spotlight

Be Flexible and Prioritize the Customer

Stacey Ackerman
Agilify Coaching & Training, Founder

Through her twenty-plus years of experience in industry and as one of the premier trainers in Agile Marketing, Stacey Ackerman knows first-hand the value of always prioritizing the customer and their needs: "[Corporations] that maintain the customers' priorities are often the ones that find the most success. On the other hand, those whose products or services are not grounded in the customer experience are likely to find it more difficult to survive." Ackerman stresses that although this view is especially apt to her sphere in Agile marketing, it is also quite pertinent to anyone looking to embark on an Agile transformation.

To illustrate, Ackerman first uses a marketing example: "Traditionally, in marketing, there's a very bureaucratic process. There's a formalized and detailed plan that can outline up to a five-year campaign." Ackerman understands that this traditional process contradicts the Agile Manifesto and, instead, ensures that her teams stay flexible and "rather base our decisions on our customers' reactions to a campaign than stick to our initial plans at all costs," in line with the Agile value, "responding to change over following a plan."

Although a marketing example, Ackerman sees a straightforward correspondence to other functions, verticals, and departments: "Regardless of what you're planning or what you're doing, you need to be flexible and able to respond as the market and customers' needs change." Ackerman cites that the accelerating rate of disruption in today's day and age is all the more reason to internalize this idea.

Similarly, Ackerman states that "those who are unable to do so will have quite a tough time keeping up with the smaller, more nimble market newcomers." The advent of disruption is a reality of today and a trend that will only continue to proliferate. Corporations must be able to adapt; Ackerman believes the easiest way is to remain flexible, keep customers' needs at the forefront, and respond as necessary.

> "If it doesn't deliver value to the customer early and continuously, then it's not Agile."
>
> **David Fisher**, *North Highland*

Embracing this mindset is easier said than done as customer needs are constantly changing. To stay abreast of their needs, consider using focus groups, surveys, community forums, and other forms of public outreach. Stacey Ackerman of Agilify Coaching & Training has the same outlook, stating, "We would much rather base our decisions on our customers' reactions to a campaign than stick to our initial plans at all costs." The core value of the Agile Manifesto, "responding to change over following a plan," further echoes this mindset.

Another way to keep up with changing customer demands is by using big data and analytics. For example, some organizations are implementing simple sentiment analysis tools to better understand customers' reactions and emotions toward shifts in a product's features or offerings. Others have leveraged analytics to predict future wants and/or needs.

> "We would much rather base our decisions on our customers' reactions to a campaign than stick to our initial plans at all costs."
>
> **Stacey Ackerman**, *Agilify Coaching & Training*

However you decide to keep up with rapidly changing customer needs, understand that nothing is as effective as empowering your teams to interface directly with customers. This allows teams to get feedback from the source in an iterative fashion. Ensure, however, that the teams are proactive in obtaining this feedback. As customers feel heard and valued, they will in turn provide more direct and honest feedback, more often, further propelling you to corporate agility.

Retrospective
Agilesson 4: Work Wisely

 START

- Streamlining processes and simplifying documentation to maximize the amount of work not done

- Identifying and piloting Agile within leading groups that will more easily adopt the methodology

- Garnering tangible results and learning from the pilot group – then, scaling Agile along with the learnings across the corproation

- Utilizing focus groups, surveys, and other forms of public outreach to stay in touch with your customers

STOP / AVOID

- Using technology as a means to short-cut your way to simplicity; these tools are powerful when used correctly

- Scaling too rapidly without learning from your initial pilot group and understanding how to apply the learnings

- Utilizing rigid marketing or product plans that do not adapt to the inevitably changing needs of your customers

QUESTIONS

- What are the areas in which you can begin simplying processes and documentation and how can you achieve it?

- How will you identify your leading group, typically comprised of those who are quick to change, flexible, and adaptable?

- Once you have piloted Agile, how will you scale your learnings to the rest of the corporation?

- How will you ensure that your teams are continuously keeping your customers' needs at the forefront?

Agilesson 5:

Measure with Meaning

Measure, monitor, and track your corporation's progress toward achieving its strategic objectives, doing Agile, and being agile. As the transformation progresses, assess your strategic objectives and the associated metrics to ensure their currency and relevance.

Why Measure?

Use metrics to measure transformation activities and to gauge your progress on your path to corporate agility.

Metrics are used across most aspects of life. Use cases occur, often unknowingly, in daily routines. To illustrate, let's return to the runner analogy from Chapters 2 and 3. With support from the coach, the runner prepares by building a training plan, outlining a schedule that ramps up over time. With this plan, day by day, the runner gets a bit stronger and runs a bit farther. Before realizing it, a marathon becomes a breeze. This would not be possible without metrics, however. Without tracking pace and distance, the runner would not know definitively if they were improving and progressing toward their overall goal or understand daily progress.

Assessing corporate agility and truly making progress toward your organizational aspirations is no different from our runner. Copious metrics exist to paint a picture of progress and performance, but be thoughtful of the metrics you use. To do this, ask yourself three leading questions:

- How do I know I'm progressing toward strategic objectives?
- How do I know I'm doing Agile?
- How do I know I'm being agile?

Selecting the correct metrics requires care and judiciousness. Although this may seem obvious and straightforward, corporations often falter in this regard. Too many metrics create confusion, add unnecessary organizational burden, come with a greater risk of being less than optimal, uninformative, and unactionable, or just measure the wrong things.

Avoid using the wrong metrics by collaborating with your team to identify only the necessary metrics that will accurately indicate the progress you're making toward your goals. Once you've landed on the correct few metrics, establish an accurate baseline, akin to how our runner recorded a baseline speed, time, and cardio status on day one. The importance of gathering a baseline cannot be overstated. Without a clear picture of where you're starting, it is difficult to evaluate the rate of your progress. As alluded to throughout the book, the path to corporate agility is long and arduous; the right metrics will facilitate fact-based conversations and enable prudent decision-making along the way. Steven Ma, an agilist who has helped businesses across the world jump start their Agile transformations, emphasizes the importance of baselining: "It requires focused intent to establish agile maturity and return-on-investment baseline measures; but when you do, you can truly understand your current state and are enabled to make continuous improvements to it."

No matter the metrics you select to track progress, know that metrics will provide a useful perspective only if monitored, reported, and kept current. Crawfurd Hill emphasizes the importance of keeping a pulse on metrics, explaining that if they are not kept current, "metrics will become just vanity. Just wrong. Not truthful." To avoid this, consider identifying resources that can help augment this process.

> "It requires focused intent to establish agile maturity and return-on-investment baseline measures; but when you do, you can truly understand your current state and are enabled to make continuous improvements to it."
>
> **Steven Ma**, *No Moss Consulting*

In a 2019 Big Data and AI Executive Survey, distributed by NewVantage Partners, only 47% of C-suite leaders at some of the largest companies in the United States indicated that data is being treated as a business asset.[1] In a world where numerous automation tools are available to streamline data capture consistently and effectively, data most certainly should be considered an asset. Automation tools and other software are storing data at a near-zero cost, a fairly recent reality. They enable corporations to analyze and standardize massive amounts of data in near real-time. By having such large capacity to store data, corporations can gather and store oceans of data. By doing this, corporations will have a repository to turn to for nearly any metric that they may want to leverage in the future for when metrics change or when strategic objectives shift. Having a historical source of truth will enable future decisions to potentially be more compelling.

Corporate Data Readiness

C-suite executives responded to a survey on data usage.

47%
View data as a business asset

31%
Developed data-driven organizations

Source: Data from NewVantage Partners, 2020[3]

Having such large amounts of data can often make insights or decisions difficult to decipher. Through the use of easy-to-read dashboards or visualizations, stakeholders can identify actionable insights, enabling near-real-time decision making, an option not available even a few years ago. Take advantage of this and other emerging technologies to forge forward on your path to corporate agility.

> "Metrics will become just vanity. Just wrong. Not truthful."
>
> **Crawfurd Hill,** *Encompass Corporation*

Measuring
"Agile Performance"

Michael Piker
Philip Morris International, VP, Global Total Rewards,
Employee Relations, Agile Performance

As a seasoned Global Human Resources (HR) and People & Culture (P&C) executive, Michael Piker has led transformations, including performance strategy, total rewards, and employee relations, at leading corporations like Philip Morris International, Naspers Limited, and Lenovo. Through all of these experiences Piker found one thing to be abundantly clear: "Companies that develop performance metrics in isolation, without any input from their teams, are setting themselves up for failure."

To solve this at Philip Morris International, as the company looked to Agile in the hopes of driving their new smoke-free strategy, Piker helped lead, in two phases, a complete revamp of their performance management system. The first phase constituted research and "collaboration between some of the biggest and best companies that also found the need embark upon a similar journey."

Piker worked with leaders from Bain Consulting and leading technology companies to come up with a new agile performance management approach that cascades team-based objectives, develops desired behaviors, builds performance development capability, and revises the rating scale and calibration approach. In short, a complete change to agile performance to accelerate the business transformation at Philip Morris International. Furthermore, Piker also incorporated the idea of team-based goals as opposed to individual ones. This "gets individuals in the right mindset and helps incentivize effective communication and collaboration."

In the spirit of Agile, however, and in line with Piker's original advice, a second phase was implemented to ensure that individuals and teams across the corporation could see and provide input on the base template created in phase one. Using "voice rooms, stretch workouts, and other collaborative methods, we made sure that our team members were a part of the process and had a voice in the final product." This resulted in a performance management system that was validated, in an iterative fashion, by Piker and other leaders at Philip Morris International, and by the team members as well.

Measure Progress
Toward Strategic Objectives

Use a variety of performance indicators to
evaluate progress toward achieving transformation
strategic objectives.

"How do I know I'm progressing toward strategic objectives?" To answer
this, first understand how these objectives are identified. At the highest
level of the corporation, executives come together and focus on big-
picture goals – strategic objectives. While identifying strategic priorities
is an essential starting point, these objectives need to be distilled into
actionable activities that can be measured and evaluated. Then, by using
appropriate metrics and deducing the associated insights, corporations
can better understand their progress toward strategic goals. However,
selecting the correct metrics to garner descriptive data and drive
prescriptive insights is not a walk in the park.

Value-Driver Tree
Consider using value-driver trees to break down your objectives into
actionable items.

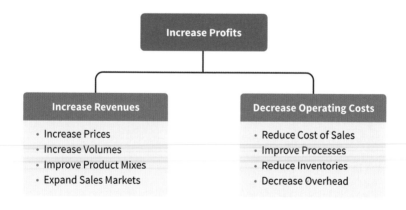

Source: DayBlink, 2020

To augment this process, consider using value-driver trees. These graphs showcase how your corporation's strategic objectives can be incrementally cascaded into smaller, more actionable ones. Take the tree on the previous page, which showcases how an example corporation's overarching objective could be to "increased profit." This objective is not very actionable on its own. However, when it is split into smaller, more specific ones – increased revenue and decreased operating costs – teams can more easily identify metrics that might align better with the specific value that they are responsible for driving. This helps teams avoid just measuring the strategic goals themselves, an often non-optimal way to work.

Furthermore, consider incorporating your value-driver tree across four major objective categories: financial, customer, people, and social. In doing so, corporations create a holistic and balanced view of their strategic objectives, accounting for the various perspectives that make up the enterprise. Countless metrics abound for each of these categories, but below are some of the ones used commonly in Agile environments.

Financial Metrics

Typically the most straightforward, measuring success through financial and economic analysis, these metrics should target the business value being delivered by the Agile teams – value to spend, OPEX, CAPEX, ROI, and throughput.

Customer Metrics

Track and evaluate customer sentiment. A major Agile component is prioritizing the customer relationship and improving their experience and satisfaction, so include metrics that focus on the customer's experience – customer satisfaction, customer churn rate, customer renewal rate, customer retention cost, CLV, and NPS.

People Metrics

Focus on your employees and the value that Agile is bringing to them. Agile is a people-centric approach, so it's critical to include metrics that focus specifically on your people – employee satisfaction, turnover ratios, and engagement scores.

Social Metrics

Measure the corporate social responsibility (CSR) of your organization. CSR metrics can span a variety of areas, including ethics, accountability, governance, community involvement, environmental protection, and more.[3] Sample metrics include average number of ethics violations in a specific time period, percent volunteer involvement, average annual community donations, and waste emissions ratios.

OKRs, first used at the Intel Corporation, also represent aggressive goals and outline measurable steps in achieving those goals.[4] OKRs, along with each metric from the four categories above, can oftentimes be confusing and burdensome. Evaluate each meticulously by using the value-driver tree. However, it will not always be a comprehensive answer. Take a further step and ask yourself, "Does this really measure progress toward the strategic objectives?" If the answer is no, it is likely not worth reporting on. Too often corporations track meaningless metrics and continue to add more. Avoid this trap!

Are You Doing Agile?

Gather and evaluate Agile metrics to create an
unbiased assessment of your ability to do Agile.

"How do I know I'm doing Agile?" Start by looking to the metrics the framework or toolkit you are utilizing provides. Then, begin to branch out to other metrics that are included under the Agile umbrella. Be wary, though. Some corporations will over-index these metrics and use them as a crutch to measure progress toward strategic objectives. Choose carefully and ensure you have separate metrics for this.

Spotlight

Identify a Goal and Measure Progress

Kishore Koduri
Ameren, Director, Enterprise Architecture, Resilience and Agile Office

Kishore Koduri, an accomplished thought leader in the Agile space, has extensive leadership experience in multiple domains, including supply chain, ERP systems, application development, among many others. Through his twenty-three-plus years of experience he has found one thing to be abundantly clear: "When implementing Agile, it's paramount that you leverage metrics to understand how well you're doing and if any adjustments need to be made."

Koduri practices what he preaches. Using the Net Promoter Score (NPS) framework, Koduri and his team were able to achieve a 70-point increase, suggesting a huge improvement in customer satisfaction. Koduri stresses, however, that you must make sure that you are utilizing the right metrics that support your goals. "We prioritized NPS because our objective was to improve our customer satisfaction. If your goal is to realize something else, make sure you're utilizing a different metric to do so."

Koduri also stresses that whichever metric you chose, ensure you stick with the metric long enough to discern a statistically significant trend. This is not to say, however, that corporations should stick with metrics that clearly are not able to gauge what they are trying to drive, but rather to understand that "trends are built off historical data. Ensure that you have enough of that data to accurately track the trend."

Koduri experienced this first hand. Take, for example, the 70-point swing in NPS discussed earlier, which took place over the course of three years. During the first, the score was mostly stagnant and, consequently, Koduri received "a lot of pushback and a lot of heat from leadership as we were not able to move the needle quickly. But I knew that this was the right metric to track, so we stuck with it. Obviously, it paid off in the end."

This is not to say, however, that traditional Agile metrics should be dismissed and downplayed; in fact, they are still valuable in gauging your teams' Agile ways of working. Remember, though, there are a lot out there. Simplify and streamline by analyzing, assessing, and choosing the metrics that work best for you. To start, consider some of these common Agile metrics.

Burndown Charts

Burndown charts are a useful metric for Scrum teams when gauging progress during a Sprint or a longer period. These charts give a graphical representation of completed story points (units of work) and story points left to go. This makes it instantly clear how much value a Sprint (or longer period) has delivered and approximately how far the team is from completing their commitment.

Velocity

Velocity is used in Scrum and identifies the average number of story points completed over a period of time, usually a Sprint. By using historical data to gauge velocity, capacity predictions can be made for future Sprints. Note, however, that comparing velocity across teams is dangerous because points are estimated relative to a team. It is, however, productive to look at the relative trends of velocity between teams to gauge how much faster a team may be improving.

Cumulative Flow

Cumulative Flow is a Kanban metric used to show status on assigned tasks. Through the simple measure and the associated visualizations, you can rapidly identify bottlenecks within your workflow. Additionally, it tracks all the different items in progress, and their duration in that state, to get a well-rounded understanding of the timeliness on certain tasks.

Spotlight

Common Language and Leading Indicators

Steve Elliott
Atlassian, Head of Jira Align

Steve Elliott, former Agilecraft founder and seasoned software executive, stresses that "when implementing Agile in any corporation, certain guardrails must be set in place to secure the transformation's sustained success." Based on a twenty-plus year career, he has identified quite a few guardrails. Foremost among them, Elliott believes, is setting up an aligned Agile terminology.

To explain further, corporations that utilize a common language can likely realize operational efficiencies. Elliott underscores this sentiment: "If everyone calls an initiative an 'initiative,' and quantifies an initiative's magnitude on the same relative scale, teams and leaders will be better able to prioritize and work together to realize that initiative." Shared terminology also extends to the software and tools a company uses. It's well known that Agile has deprioritized tools as a main driver for success, but standardizing the software a corporation leverages can still help augment and bolster processes along the way.

Another guardrail is the notion that if a corporation is to invest in a feature or capability, that "investment has to tie back to a leading indicator or some measure of success." Obviously, not every feature or capability can cleanly tie back to a metric, but Elliott believes that if this requirement is at least voiced and heard, it starts to drive the mindset of not just doing work for the sake of work, but to drive business outcomes for the corporation.

As with most aspects of an Agile transformation, in order to ensure these guardrails are understood and internalized by all, Elliott stresses that executives and leaders must communicate them early and often. Done correctly, the aforementioned guardrails, among others, can help corporations implement Agile effectively and efficiently.

Being Agile

Measure with your mind, but also hear with
your heart.

Throughout this chapter, you've already answered the two questions that
are often most discussed and utilized by corporate executives. And, while
they are definitely important and necessary, the last question deserves an
equal place in gauging progress on your Agile journey: "How do I know
I'm being agile?"

This question is important because it looks deeper than the quantifi-
able data and metrics you've established from the first two questions. It's
something that you committed to back in Chapter 2 when starting on
this journey – being agile. Yes, the need to commit to corporate agility
and becoming adaptive, collaborative, rapid, and transparent arose from
something else, from the need to achieve your strategic objectives in the
face of timeless disruption. Do not forget, however, what you wanted to
become (be agile) when you started on this journey.

To answer this question, corporations need to define a different type
of metric. Yes, there are the traditional means – surveys, interviews, NPS,
Customer Satisfaction Score (CSAT), etc. – to measure these adjectives,
but these are often not enough to identify if you are truly instilling
corporate agility into your people and corporation. You will need to, in
addition to metrics and data, utilize heart, feeling, and intuition. You'll
need to, as discussed in Chapter 5, be on the ground and talk to your
team. These are the important things that seem to have been lost over
time to sentiments like "if it can't be measured, it can't be managed." NPS
and CSAT can be helpful and insightful, but these "measurable" metrics
can be gamed and falsified. So, measure with your mind, of course. But,
don't discount what your heart is telling you with regard to being agile.

Spotlight

Listen with Your Heart

Joseph Murray, Ph.D
DayBlink Consulting, Partner

Joseph Murray is an executive and management consultant with extensive experience in the telecommunications and media sectors, specializing in digital strategy, planning and execution, operational excellence, among others. Prior to joining DayBlink Consulting as a Partner, Murray helped lead and deliver numerous large-scale business transformation programs at companies across the globe while with Ericsson Consulting, KPMG, Deloitte Consulting, and AT&T. Murray also has a Ph.D. in Operations Research from the University of Michigan.

Throughout his career, Murray has experienced first-hand the advent of technology and data in the workplace. He believes that the proliferation of this trend has given corporations the tools to measure every aspect of their business efficiently and effectively: "Big Data. Emergent Technology. Advanced Analytics. Over the years, corporations have become increasingly dependent on them, and rightfully so."

While Murray believes this "dependency" has enabled corporations to rise to new heights, he also stresses the idea that some leaders and management teams have begun to over-index on the idea, neglecting a different form of measurement that Murray finds is crucial: listen and assess with your heart. He feels that "the advanced tools we have available today always deserve a seat at the table. However, leaders also need to allocate some capacity to being on the ground, interacting with your teams, and seeing for yourself."

Murray finds this idea is especially important in the context of Agile transformations: "You're asking your teams to fundamentally think and act differently. This is one of the areas in which all the data in the world may not be enough. You'll need to employ a different approach to understand if your teams have changed." Murray emphasizes that corporations and leaders who are able to find the intersection of these two different ways of measuring are those likely to find great success.

Monitor Your Objectives

Continuously assess and adjust measurements
to maintain alignment with your corporation's
strategic objectives.

If you want to get in better shape, you can use metrics to gauge progress toward your goal in heart rate, calories burned, etc. However, if this goal is deprioritized or changed, you must start measuring a different metric to track your progress toward something else. Similarly, when you begin your path to corporate agility, you will have a set of strategic objectives you want to achieve and desired characteristics you want to embody. When these objectives change and your desired characteristics follow suit, you cannot continue to use the metrics you first put in place. Instead, assess and adapt to ensure you're using metrics that allow you to gauge progress toward your current goals.

Take, for example, the coronavirus disease (COVID-19) pandemic. Prior to the mass lockdown of cities and travel restrictions around the world, most corporations' reported strategic objectives centered on growth opportunities, financial or otherwise. When the pandemic came about, however, life as we knew it changed drastically. These very same companies that were so focused on penetrating new markets just a few weeks prior, needed to shift priorities, focusing instead on retaining their current ones. This example is obviously a dramatic one, but the lesson is apt. As discussed extensively in Chapter 1, change is ever-recurrent and your strategic objectives will shift. Your ways of measuring must also adapt alongside.

Let's look at another example. Prior to 2007, Netflix primarily focused on creating topline revenue. However, Netflix's transition from a bundled platform to two separate services – mail order DVDs and online streaming, in conjunction with raising their membership fee by 60%, led to the loss of hundreds of thousands of customers.[5] Having alienated their member base, Netflix realigned its strategic objectives and chose to refocus on customer retention rather than topline revenue. They reverted to a simplified platform and eventually regained the interest and trust of customers. After two years of hard work their stock price rebounded to an all-time high of almost $400 per share in October 2013.[6]

In summary, standardize on a select set of performance indicators across the organization to understand your progress toward your goals and toward corporate agility. This also provides an ancillary benefit, enabling your corporation to be more adaptable and able to pivot in the face of disruptions, external forces, and changing forcing functions.

Retrospective

Agilesson 5: Measure with Meaning

 START

- Establishing baseline measurements for your metrics to understand where you are in your journey and how you can improve

- Utilizing value-driver trees or other tools to help identify the metrics that help gauge progress toward your strategic objectives

- Using core Agile metrics as a means of understanding how well your teams are working in Agile

- Continuously assessing and monitoring your metrics to maintain alignment with your inevitably changing strategic objectives

 STOP / AVOID

- Utilizing too many metrics as this often creates confusion and adds unnecessary organizational burden

- Over-indexing on core Agile metrics as a means to measure progress toward strategic objectives

- Measuring only with your mind; instead, also measure with heart, feeling, and intuition to gauge your team in regard to being agile

QUESTIONS

- How will you measure progress toward strategic objectives and update those measurements as objectives inevitably change?

- How will you leverage core Agile metrics to understand how well your teams are doing Agile?

- How will you balance the use of data and metrics with measuring with heart, feeling, and intuition?

CHAPTER 10

Agilesson 6:

Forge Forward

Look at common behaviors and trends that indicate if Agile is taking root within your corporation. Then, look to other methodologies that can coexist with Agile. Similar to Agile, these methodologies are unique and powerful in their own right. Find the one, or the combination, that works for you.

Is Agile Business as Usual?

Identify whether Agile has become the norm
within the corporation.

Every enterprise's path to corporate agility is different. Corporations have different strategic objectives, products and services, desired characteristics, geographies, cultures, frameworks, toolkits, metrics, and more. But what should be shared across all corporations seeking corporate agility is the central idea of being agile. In the previous chapter, we discussed both being agile and doing Agile. When both of these combine, and the mindset becomes unified, executives can truly derive a path to where Agile becomes the new normal – values and principles lived out each and every day.

While this may seem like a simple directive, getting to the point where being agile and doing Agile converge will be a difficult task for any leadership team. But there are some telltale signs that can be used to gauge if your corporation is trending toward corporate agility. Below we list some core behaviors that are common to Agile teams and corporations. If you see these happening within your enterprise, know you are making progress toward corporate agility.

- **Engage Customers:** Work with stakeholders throughout the product development process and react positively to feedback. Ensure customers are involved throughout the process.
- **Improve Continuously:** Consistently and swiftly iterate on products to ensure they are of top quality when customers use them. Teams and individuals approach every day with a "Kaizen" mindset, whether it be for their individual skills or team-wide processes.
- **Organize Autonomously:** Self-organize and have a cadence for important events and meetings. Teams must be both cross-functional and collaborative in a flat, non-hierarchical,

transparent structure, emphasizing the importance of creating quality products without heavy documentation.

- **Prioritize Functionality**: Recognize the importance of product delivery that is satisfactory, but know that there will be iterations to take it to the next level. Communicate face-to-face and collaborate often to ensure the message and directives are clear and effective.
- **Emphasize Feedback**: Gather feedback from your customers and stakeholders. All members collaborate and contribute, regardless of their position. Discuss feedback and incorporate it into your processes and products to meet the expectations of customers and stakeholders.
- **Integrate Technology**: Leverage the capabilities of modern technology to minimize the amount of unnecessary work. Provide and create products at an expeditious rate. Leverage real-time metrics and share them in an easily digestible manner.

While the above considerations are important in identifying if Agile has been adopted by teams, the proliferation of another trend can also be a leading indicator. Since Agile is about people, focusing on their engagement is prudent. Successful corporations often find themselves analyzing team NPS.

Before deep-diving into it, a little bit about NPS. Originally created in 2003 by Fred Reichheld, a partner at Bain & Company, to measure how well an organization generates loyal advocates, it has grown to capture several other insights.[1] Since its genesis, thousands of innovative companies have used the metric, and adapted and expanded on the initial structure. In today's world, it is primarily used to gauge a specific corporation's external customer loyalty.[2] It additionally is used within corporations to track a team's contentment and comfort with initiatives or changes, including Agile implementations.

Its calculation can be intricate but, at a high level, is simple enough. The question "How likely are you to recommend Agile from zero to ten?" is asked of all team members. Then, those who answered nine or ten (promoters), those who answered seven or eight (passives), and those who scored six or lower (detractors) are separated. The final step of the calculation requires you to take your percentage of detractors and subtract it from your percent of promoters, leading to a final score between –100 and 100. To give a frame of reference on what your score means, see the graph below.

NPS Scale

NPS can gauge the collective sentiment of a particular group.

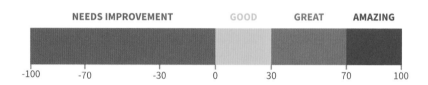

Source: Adapted from Retently, 2020[3]

Understand, however, that the score is relative to your industry, your department, and your team. A more insightful data point is not necessarily the score itself, but, as alluded to above, its trend. A trend in NPS can provide insight into a variety of different aspects, with many studies showing strong correlation with other metrics (revenue, engagement, etc.). However, unbeknownst to many, the trend of your NPS can tell you much about whether Agile has become business as usual (BAU) within your teams and your corporation, though maybe not intuitively.

To explain, DayBlink Consulting mined and normalized data from its clients, across multiple geographies and industries. The results suggest that, when Agile teams are launched, team NPS rises swiftly. Given the people-centric nature of Agile, this should come as no surprise. Some attributed it to the halo effect of implementing Agile. And this makes sense. Teams are often willing and ready, excited right out of the gate to see results. DayBlink often saw, however, that over the course of time, the halo effect diminished, gradually decreasing NPS. Some may interpret these metrics to say "Agile isn't working."

However, it's quite the opposite. The decreasing trend actually suggests Agile is becoming the new normal and ingrained in the individuals' and corporate culture. Teams that experienced this trend would objectively do Agile and be more agile.

NPS Case Study

The initial "halo" effect gradually diminishes over time as reflected with the NPS.

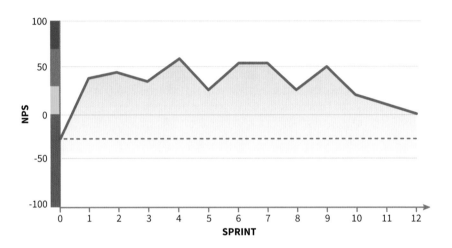

Source: DayBlink, 2020

This is not to say, however, that your NPS will decline forever. If it does, then a serious issue is likely occurring, necessitating a deeper evaluation of what is happening within that specific team. It is important to note that even with the NPS gradual decline and stabilization, the engagement of the team usually rests well above the pre-Agile baseline. Once the NPS levels off, review the considerations discussed earlier in the chapter as the utilization of both can help you identify if Agile has become the norm.

Spotlight

Achieving Executive Buy-In Through a Hybrid Approach

Crawfurd Hill
Encompass Corporation, Corporate Agility Director

Through his extensive experience in leading large-scale Agile transformations across numerous corporations and industries, Crawfurd Hill found that the most significant determinant to a successful transformation is executive buy-in. Hill stresses, however, that "gaining this buy-in, while crucial, is often far more difficult than anyone expects it to be."

While working with teams across digital innovation, communications, marketing, and e-commerce spaces, Hill found that, no matter the industry, executives can be reluctant to take transformations seriously, and, instead, avoid them entirely as it prompts discomfort in their current roles, positions in which they find security and comfort. Hill believes some leaders "go as far as to say Agile is not a framework to get stuff done."

To help leaders and executives circumvent this mindset, Hill employs a few tactics to train and coach them during a corporation's Agile journey, ensuring they are brought along. One tactic Hill finds to be successful is to gradually integrate aspects of Agile into other methodologies that are already established and already in use across the enterprise. In doing so, executive concerns regarding the efficacy of Agile are often quelled as they see it work in harmony with already established ways of working. Furthermore, by incorporating a mix of methodologies – for example, Agile, Design Thinking, and Lean – Hill believes that corporations can realize synergistic value – in this case, a flow of innovation that was not achievable before. This integration process can be further supported by using Agile frameworks that already incorporate the principles and processes of other methodologies, like Scrumban, Lean Agile, and others.

The combinations are vast, as Agile, especially the values, principles, and themes inherent, can be paired or overlaid with most methodologies to create an effective hybrid approach. Hill emphasizes, however, that whichever combination you choose, ensure the executive team is comfortable with the approach: remember, without executive buy-in, any attempt at corporate agility can and will likely fail.

Agile Plays Nice

Utilize Agile with other methodologies to
realize synergistic value and further drive
your strategic objectives.

As discussed in Chapter 3, Agile can be thought of in two ways: being agile, which denotes the core values, principles, and mindsets of Agile, and doing Agile, which represents the structures and processes. And, while both combined equate to the powerful Agile frameworks and toolkits detailed throughout the book, there is ample opportunity to be agile in conjunction with other ways of working. To explain further, let's recall the twelve principles of the Agile Manifesto. When read independently, these principles do not need to describe Agile environments. In fact, you can often apply them in non-Agile, even Waterfall, ways of working.

For example, measure success through working software to improve customer satisfaction in your Waterfall environments. Alternatively, many corporations transition to co-location to increase collaboration and transparency in their Design Thinking teams. Or, consider utilizing a continuous improvement or "Kaizen" mindset to augment your Six Sigma processes, continually striving to achieve and surpass the six-standard-deviation threshold.

As discussed, although being agile and doing Agile can be complementary, not every corporation can work in this manner. Sometimes, enterprises already operating in traditional methodologies cannot allocate the time, effort, and resources required for a large-scale transformation. In these cases, adopt Agile mindsets, values, and principles to augment your current processes.

As Agile becomes BAU and your corporation has truly internalized being agile and doing Agile, you will likely see that either coexists well with other improvement methodologies that you're also using in your transformation journey. Agile is accretive and can take on aspects of other approaches and become even more unique to you. Agile is also synergistic – other methodologies you're using will improve by taking on aspects of Agile. And that's part of the power and attraction – being agile permeates the corporation; it is a rising tide that can lift other boats. The following is a brief overview of some of these methodologies in the current transformation landscape. Keep in mind, however, that this is an evolving list. As new methodologies emerge, they will replace, augment, or integrate with the current methodologies.

Combining Methodologies

Utilize Agile in conjunction with other methodologies to garner synergistic value.

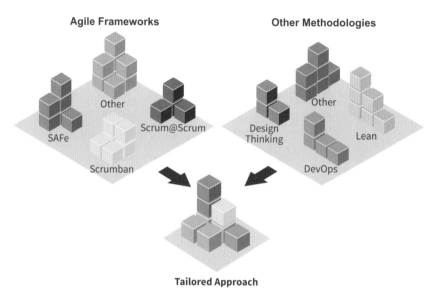

Business Process Reengineering

Popularized in 1990 by MIT professor Michael Hammer, Business Process Reengineering (BPR) focuses on breaking down an organization's main processes, then rebuilding them ground up to develop best practices and superior operations.[4] Said differently, this methodology is used to overhaul the design of certain processes, making them leaner and more efficient.

Over time, however, an overemphasis on cost reduction and quality improvement resulted in misuses of the framework. Companies began implementing this methodology as an excuse to downsize. Negative press

Transformation Methodologies

Agile, one of many options to achieve corporate agility, works well when requirements are unknown and actions are unclear.

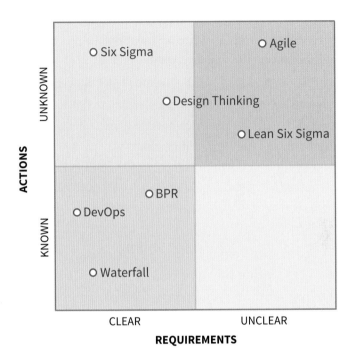

ensued, and, as such, BPR garnered a negative connotation in recent years. However, companies that focus on the core aspects of the methodology – refocusing values to meet customer demands, reducing costs and cycle times, improving product and service quality, reorganizing into cross-functional teams, and redesigning and improving processes across the company[5] – are still finding success. This fundamental overhaul of processes requires much time, effort, planning, and money. Tallyfy, a workflow software, breaks down how to implement BPR into four distinct steps:[6]

- **Identify and Communicate the Need for Change:** Convince others why making the change is essential for the company; this is not hard when your enterprise isn't doing well. Often, however, you need to show the organization isn't doing as well as it could.

- **Put Together a Team of Experts**: Gather a team of skilled people, usually composed of Senior Managers, Operational Managers, and Reengineering Experts.
- **Find Inefficient Processes and Define KPIs**: Define Key Performance Indicators (KPIs), then use business process mapping to identify the processes to optimize.
- **Reengineer Processes and Compare KPIs**: Implement a redesigned process on a small scale. Evaluate your changes through KPIs; if they show improvement, incrementally scale the solution to the rest of the enterprise.

Waterfall

This methodology was first introduced in a 1970 article written by software developer Winston W. Royce, who, ironically enough, introduced it as a flawed, non-working model.[7] Nevertheless, the software industry was quick to adopt this approach of "moving onto a phase of development only after the previous one was completed in its entirety," formally referring to it as the Waterfall model, which can be categorized into a six-stage process:[8]

- **Plan:** Gather requirements from customers, sales department, market surveys, and domain experts.
- **Define:** Document and define the product requirements and get them approved from the customer or market analysts. This is done through a Software Requirement Specification (SRS).
- **Design:** Create multiple approaches for the product architecture; document this in a Design Document Specification (DDS).
- **Build:** Develop and build the product using the DDS. Ensure adherence to the coding guidelines defined by the organization and programming tools.
- **Test:** Report, track, fix, and retest product defects until the product reaches the quality standards as defined in the SRS.

- **Deploy:** Release the product into the appropriate market. Then, periodically perform maintenance for the existing customer base.

Although Waterfall's detailed plans are meant to improve the overall quality of the product and streamline the development process itself, it oftentimes leads to delays in delivery and unmet customer needs. Many agilists argue that the Waterfall approach is now unsuited to today's environment of accelerating change, and instead choose Agile, which many believe to be the antithesis of Waterfall. However, though controversial in Agile circles, some corporations can find, in certain circumstances, success when using them together. These occurrences happen often when large, traditional enterprises, with Waterfall baked into their processes, do not have the capabilities to completely transition into Agile. They will, instead, use an Agile-Waterfall hybrid in the interim before completely transitioning to Agile afterwards.

Design Thinking

Dating back to the 1950s, Design Thinking has undergone many transformations over the years. Originally utilized in architecture and engineering, it has since been adopted by a wide group of entrepreneurs, businesses, and industries.[9] At a basic level, Design Thinking reframes problems in a human-centric way and leads to more innovative solutions to meet customers' needs. The methodology has five central stages:[10]

- **Empathize:** Gain an empathetic understanding of the problem you're trying to solve. This step is crucial as it allows you to gain real insight through the lenses of the users.
- **Define:** Analyze and synthesize your observations to define the core problems.
- **Ideate:** "Think outside the box" and look for alternative or innovative ways to solve the problem statement.

- **Prototype:** Experiment and identify the best solution for the problems you've identified in the first three stages through prototypes.
- **Test:** Explore the best solution identified in the prototype phase. This step is an iterative process and the results are often used to redefine or evolve the problem statement.

Many large corporations effectively leverage Design Thinking with Agile. Oftentimes, companies will implement the two together to produce synergistic benefits. Others that already have a Design Thinking process find transitioning to Agile is a natural course of action.[11,12]

Six Sigma

Six Sigma is a disciplined, data-driven approach that drives quality and process improvements to achieve an operational benchmark. Its comprehensive definition is a mouthful: a process in which "99.99966%, or six standard deviations, of all opportunities to produce some feature are expected to be free of defects."[13] The methodology is described by Simplilearn Solutions, an educational training company, in five key principles:[14]

- **Focus on the Customer:** Establish a standard of quality by understanding your customers, their needs, and what drives sales or loyalty.
- **Measure the Value Stream:** Map the steps in your processes to determine areas of improvement. Collect data on those areas to determine the underlying cause.
- **Get Rid of the Junk:** Change the identified processes to eliminate variation and remove defects by removing activities that do not add customer value.
- **Keep the Ball Rolling:** Incorporate specialized training and knowledge transfer so all members within the organization are proficient in Six Sigma, ensuring its continued success.

- **Ensure a Flexible and Responsive Ecosystem**: Instill a culture of flexibility and responsiveness so implementation of process change is streamlined.

In 1995, when Jack Welch, then CEO of General Electric, made Six Sigma a core tenet of his business strategy, the methodology gained widespread popularity as the term became synonymous with corporate success. GE spent $1 billion-plus on training its employees across all business units. From accounting to call centers to customer service, every GE department developed tools designed to reduce variation in production processes.[15]

Over the years, Six Sigma became the gold standard for improving customer satisfaction and operational efficiency. The sheen faded, however, as GE's performance declined. Six Sigma further fell out of favor as companies began prioritizing innovation over reducing variability. In recent years, however, Six Sigma has seen a resurgence, especially in call centers.[16]

Lean

An evolution of the production system introduced by Toyota, the Lean methodology enables corporations to improve their flexibility and efficiency. Although it started in manufacturing, over the years it has gained popularity around the world in almost every industry and sector.[17] The methodology itself is guided by two overarching tenets: respect for people and continuous improvement. Furthermore, it practices five core principles:[18]

- **Identify Value**: Start with your customers, as they determine where the value in a product is, not the producer. Specify how this value appears in your processes.
- **Map the Value Stream**: Understand the products' complete life cycle to identify and eliminate waste and achieve increased efficiency. Ensure each process is carefully analyzed and assessed.

- **Create Flow:** Ensure a smooth flow through the value stream as a lack thereof will result in waste. Understand, however, that not all waste can be eliminated. Consider the law of diminishing returns in regard to the effort required to reduce more.
- **Establish Pull:** Do not create value ahead of time. Instead, wait for the customer to ask for or "pull" the product. Upon the customer doing so, begin producing the product. This minimizes delivery cycle time and increases flexibility.
- **Seek Perfection:** Now that you've considered the other four principles, start it over again. Continuously strive to perfect and achieve an increasingly lean process.

Lean is often considered a main competitor to Agile, especially when Kanban is used as the Agile framework, as they share many similarities. Remember, however, one does not necessarily have to choose between the two.

DevOps

As the world moves away from traditional, siloed methodologies like Waterfall, and toward more continuous workflows, the need to combine or integrate development and deployment has increased. DevOps, which stands for development and operations, is a practice that aims to do this, merging development, quality assurance, and operations into a single, continuous set of processes.[19] DevOps is centered around five main principles:[20]

- **Customer-Centric Action:** Have the guts to continuously innovate, pivot when a strategy doesn't work, and constantly invest in products and solutions that satisfy the customer.
- **Create with the End in Mind:** Let go of Waterfall and process-oriented models; instead, work as product companies that focus on building working solutions.
- **End-to-End Responsibility:** Organize teams vertically so that they are fully accountable from inception to deployment.

- **Cross-Functional Autonomous Teams:** Ensure a comprehensive set of skills on your vertically organized, fully responsible teams so they can be fully independent throughout the life cycle.
- **Continuous Improvement:** Adapt continuously in light of changing circumstances. This is necessary to minimize waste and optimize efficiency when situations inevitably change.

Teams will adhere to these principles through practices like frequent deployments, validating ideas early, and in-team collaboration to achieve benefits like continuous delivery, faster feedback, and product quality.[21] You'll notice that the DevOps practices, principles, and benefits sound similar to that of Agile. That's because the two work hand in hand, and are commonly found together in IT and other departments around the world.

When the co-authors of the Agile Manifesto cemented the values and principles into their ledger, they focused on flexibility as the preeminent way of working. When considering Agile as a way of thinking, there is more to it. The values and principles inherent are truths that can help solve for the timeless disruptions that all corporations face, regardless of the methodology they employ. Those who have fully embraced Agile as the new normal should look to implement the advantages inherent with other frameworks or toolkits, Agile or not, as they seek business agility.

Others, however, who still have some hesitation with Agile in the corporation should seek another path. For Agile to be successful, there needs to be buy-in; it needs to be a commitment to doing Agile and being agile. If your enterprise can achieve both of these, great! If you can't commit to both, consider utilizing another way of working and leveraging the aspects of Agile that work for your corporation.

Remember, this is your path, your journey to corporate agility. You need to do what makes the most sense for your corporation: try only Agile, try Agile in conjunction with one, or maybe all methodologies, or try one of these methodologies outlined above. You are a part of an exciting time for your corporation – find the best path for you to reach corporate agility.

Methodologies
that Work Together

Dave Witkin
Packaged Agile, Principal

For nearly twenty years, Dave Witkin, a leading agilist, trainer, and coach, has helped US Government Agencies realize the promise of Agile through large-scale transformations. While the market landscape changed drastically during this time, he found one thing to hold true: "The root causes supporting the need for agility are more important now than ever before."

Witkin has found that many leading ways of working require an Agile foundation. For example, he cites DevOps and Design Thinking as two popular concepts that are an expansion of what good agilists have been doing for decades. He adds that some people discuss these concepts in ways that make them sound separate, but in actuality they are completely interdependent.

To understand the synergy, Witkin points to how the values and principles of Agile underlie all methodologies. For example, "Working software over comprehensive documentation" is a critical aspect of Design Thinking, Extreme Programming, Scrum, and other frameworks and toolkits. Witkin goes on to say that working software is the best measure of progress because, "as humans we like to believe we are on-track even when we are way behind. Or when we have no feedback suggesting we're even building the right thing. So, until you have something tangible you can touch and interact with, you can't be confident in your progress. That's true when using any Agile framework."

Witkin cites another principle with wide application to be self-organizing teams. "We find that leaders often feel the need to jump in and make decisions because that's what they think they are paid to do." He argues that this view makes transparent a fundamental flaw. "If we need management to jump in and make decisions, then we probably don't have the right team in the first place. Great teams know more than management and are empowered to make decisions."

Retrospective

Agilesson 6: Forge Forward

START

- Utilizing changes in behavior and other leading indicators to understand if Agile has become ingrained within the corporation

- Understanding the halo effect and how it can also indicate some level of normality in regard to Agile

- Exploring other transformation methodologies that, when chosen thoughtfully, can work synergistically with Agile

- Finding the best path on your unique journey to corporate agility, whether it is through Agile, another methodology, or a combination of methodologies

STOP / AVOID

- Utilizing the absolute NPS from your team to gauge sentiment; instead, use the trend in scores as a more insightful data point

- Pairing being agile with doing Agile in every situation; although they can be complementary, not every corporation has the means to work in this manner

- Forcing methodologies to work with one another; remember, they are often synergistic together, but can still be powerful alone

QUESTIONS

- What indicators will you look for to understand if Agile has become the new norm within your corporation?

- Do you have the time, effort, and resources necessary to adapt the core values, principles, and mindsets of Agile as well as the structures and processes?

- Do you see any benefit to utilizing Agile alongside other methodologies that may provide different streams of value?

PART THREE

The Future of Agile

The timeless need for corporate agility necessitates that Agile continuously evolves. Understand where it may be headed and sprint in step.

11

The Future of Agile

Disruption, a timeless force, will continue to jolt and jar corporations, compelling them to change and transform. Agile, as a transformation approach, will continue to evolve as well.

The Agilessons Are Agile

Like Agile transformations, these Agilessons took time, effort, and a number of iterations to get just right. Months of interviews and primary and secondary research were required to tease out common threads and insights. Sticky notes covered the offices of DayBlink while stand-ups, stand-downs, backlogs, and burndown charts were all brought to bear. Volumes of data and content were amassed and carefully curated. However, the journey was worth it. Now, and in the future, executives will be able to leverage the Agilessons as a compass to navigate the tricky waters of their Agile transformation.

Agile, true to its twelfth principle, will continuously reflect on how to become more effective, then iterate and adjust accordingly. At the time of this book's publication, the Scaled Agile Framework (SAFe), for instance, has released five versions, each evolved from the previous. And there are more in the works! The Agilessons are no different. You can stay current with them and with other corporate Agile resources by visiting www.CorporateAgility.com.

All this is not to say, however, that the Agilessons will fundamentally change. Remember, the values and principles underlying Agile address challenges that are not unique to today but, rather, challenges that are timeless. Disruptions and failures, trust, team, purpose: Walt Disney needed to understand them almost a hundred years ago, as do today's executives, and as will tomorrow's. And while the nuances and details of Agile will evolve and make Agile more proficient and efficient at solving these challenges, its foundational theme will always hold true: develop working and relevant products and get them into the hands of the customers as rapidly as possible.

With that said, it's still useful to reflect on the journey ahead for Agile. Think of it as Agile's roadmap and product backlog. Understanding where Agile can and will potentially go can arm you to preemptively evolve your unique Agile approach within your enterprise and unlock ever-more business potential. The possibilities of where Agile is headed are vast and varied. That said, we asked the leading agilists and successful business executives we interviewed to provide their predictions for Agile's future, all of whom shared their interesting and insightful views. Though a few quotes attributed to individuals are highlighted herein, the corporate agility predictions were distilled and normalized from hundreds of predictions.

Corporate Agility Predictions

Agile, as a transformation approach, will continue to evolve.

Agile in Industry

- Agile use cases will expand across new markets and verticals
- Agile transformations will increase in the healthcare industry
- Private equity firms will adopt Agile to improve their portfolios
- Academia will integrate Agile into curriculums

Purpose to the People

- The role of the middle managers will continue to evolve
- Enterprises will rethink their co-location strategy
- Generational values will align with an Agile culture

Continuous Evolution

- The Agile certification bar will rise
- Emerging technologies will augment Agile at scale

Source: DayBlink, 2020

Agile in Industry

Adoption of Agile has accelerated, but this is only the beginning. Agile will continue to evolve and grow across markets and industries, within corporations, and even into the world of academia.

Use cases will expand, penetrating new verticals and emerging markets

As the benefits of Agile at scale become commonplace, corporations will continue to utilize Agile outside IT departments and expand into other parts of the organization to stay competitive in today's demanding market. As such, Agile will evolve from its original focus, and enable the transformation of any vertical or function within a corporation that values innovation and collaboration, particularly thriving in areas that are dynamic in nature.

Consider, for example, the marketing industry, which has already developed and implemented their own take on the Agile Manifesto, termed the Agile Marketing Manifesto.[1] This approach has proliferated in marketing departments across many corporations. Looking forward, as the flexibility of Agile and its use cases becomes better known, many more will follow in marketing's footsteps and adopt a modified version of Agile as a means of transforming out of their traditional ways of working. Stacey Ackerman of Agilify Coaching & Training feels the same: "We're seeing software verticals chug along, but, when the rest of the company doesn't believe in the same values, it can cause disruption. Now, we're seeing marketing, HR, and finance adopt the same ways of working, and seeing lots of success."

In addition to expanding to new verticals, Agile will also proliferate in emerging markets. This will be triggered by a race to not only survive, but grow and expand by being flexible, adaptable, and innovative. Akin to the increased adoption of Agile in Asian and European markets following their economic boom, African, Latin American, and other emerging markets will likely make the transition as well.[2]

Spotlight

Agile Across the Enterprise

Junius Rowland
AutoZone, IT Manager, Agile Delivery Office

J unius Rowland has substantiated successes in enterprise Agile transformations, information systems, and project management. Through his ten-plus years of experience helping large corporations like Aflac, L3 Technologies, and AutoZone realize increased productivity, service standards, and customer satisfaction, he has seen Agile evolve out of the IT space for which it was originally created, into all areas across the enterprise. He believes this trend will only continue to proliferate as other individuals, teams, and departments realize the potential benefits that come from working in Agile.

Corporations are built of several different departments, many of which could benefit from Agile. But, Rowland believes that certain departments are better positioned to make the transition than others. Take, for example, Human Resources and Marketing, departments Rowland believes "can especially take advantage of the fast feedback loops and quick decision-making that Agile prioritizes." As such, he believes that it may be prudent for corporations looking to scale Agile to look at these departments first.

Rowland warns, however, that those looking to scale must first understand the dependencies of the various verticals and departments. As your Agile practice grows larger and larger, "make sure you aren't losing the essence of Agile. This isn't possible if you need to suddenly wait two weeks for a decision over here, and three weeks for a decision over there."

To mitigate this known risk, Rowland suggests leaders "step back and look at the enterprise as a whole. Identify the areas where Agile can fit best, and understand the ones where paths cross the least." Rowland finds that those who take this approach are more able to successfully scale Agile as they avoid departments that may not be in the right part of their journey for Agile and, similarly, identify those that are ready to make the leap.

> "We're seeing software verticals chug along, but, when the rest of the company doesn't believe in the same values, it can cause disruption. Now, we're seeing marketing, HR, and finance adopt the same ways of working, and seeing lots of success."

Stacey Ackerman, *Agilify Coaching & Training*

Transformations will increase in the healthcare industry

Healthcare is dominated by large legacy players, riddled with bureaucracy and outdated practices. In recent years, however, companies like Intuitive Surgical, Zocdoc, and Oscar Health have taken advantage of this traditionally slow-moving industry, disrupting the healthcare status quo by providing more efficient and digitized solutions.

The success of these disruptors has forced legacy health players to respond, with some turning to Agile as the answer. Take, for example, Marcus Johnson and Highmark Health, one of the largest healthcare Integrated Delivery and Finance Systems (IDFS) in America, who has already begun to implement Agile throughout the enterprise with much success: "Our decision to go Agile was to position ourselves as a market leader. We saw the benefits and outcomes of Agile in other industries and we have used it as an opportunity to be ahead of the curve in healthcare."

> "Our decision to go Agile was to position ourselves as a market leader. We saw the benefits and outcomes of Agile in other industries and we have used it as an opportunity to be ahead of the curve in healthcare."

Marcus Johnson, *Highmark Health*

As Agile case studies in healthcare expand, enterprises will be more exposed to these innovative and flexible ways of working. In fact, a study by Bain and Company found that nearly 80% of healthcare executives say they need to be more Agile in 2019 and that 75% find their Agile teams perform better or significantly better than their traditional ones.[3] This sentiment will only continue to proliferate. The lessons from the coronavirus disease (COVID-19) pandemic will not long be forgotten. As such, corporations will prioritize an Agile way of working as new players and new crises demand flexible and adaptable solutions.[4] Those who aren't able to evolve through this way of working will have to find alternative solutions, or face the same demise as Blockbuster, Eastman Kodak, and others discussed in Chapter 1.

Private equity firms will adopt Agile to improve their portfolios

The private equity and venture capital landscapes are complex and cyclical. Traditionally, the life cycle is described in three steps: deal generation, due diligence, and ongoing ownership. This investment life cycle will stay the same for the foreseeable future; however, the steps within are intricate and dynamic. As such, numerous opportunities exist for these firms to outperform competitors by using an Agile way of working. Louis Toth, co-founder of Comcast Ventures, further underscores this sentiment: "In corporate ventures, you have to feel comfortable … spotting and delivering key trends for executives in consumable bite-sized chunks, akin to how Agile takes a very large problem and breaks it down."

With that said, the natural gateway for Agile to enter the industry is through the firms' various investments. As Agile is increasingly adopted across enterprises and industries, private equity and venture capital firms will gain exposure to Agile approaches and their successes. As such, firms will not only see Agile as a means for accelerated due diligence, enhanced investment selection, and more tactful portfolio oversight, but also as an offering to improve the synergistic value of their portfolios.

> "In corporate ventures, you have to feel comfortable … spotting and delivering key trends for executives in consumable bite-sized chunks, akin to how Agile takes a very large problem and breaks it down."
>
> **Louis Toth**, *Comcast Ventures*

Academia will integrate Agile into curriculums

In many universities around the world, Agile is slowly being introduced. For example, American University offers a Master of Science degree in Agile Project Management and Cornell University also offers a course in Agile Project Management. Other universities have followed suit. As the demand for Agile continues to increase in today's fast-paced landscape, academia must be able to continually supply that demand via classes, concentrations, and other outlets in the curriculum. At the time of publication, this is not yet the case.

Agile in Academia

Survey participants indicate a strong interest in more Agile academic offerings.

95%
Believe Agile should be an integral part of the Computer Science Curriculum

82%
Believe Agile is better learned in academia than on the job

Source: Data from Javaid Ali, 2015[3]

Sondra Ashmore, AVP and Business Partner at Berkley Technology Services LLC, believes the same: "New hires are almost exclusively learning Agile on the job. We need to help and partner with academia, especially in this day and age, to incorporate more Agile." This is further underscored by an Agile ME study that showed that 95% of respondents believed Agile should be an integral part of any computer science program and that 82% of respondents believed Agile is better learned in academia than on the job.[6]

> "New hires are exclusively learning Agile on the job. We need to help and partner with academia, especially in this day and age, to incorporate more Agile."
>
> **Sondra Ashmore,** *Berkley Technology Services LLC*

Agile will likely first take hold in the graduate setting, as it has already begun to. From there, it will cascade down to the undergraduate level, and perhaps lower as well. Understand, however, that although this sentiment is shared by most, many still have not fully aligned on when Agile should first be introduced to students. This misalignment is mostly due to one big limitation: as Agile has had little to no place in the traditional curriculum thus far, most professors have not been armed with the requisite knowledge to teach it. Furthermore, as discussed in Chapter 7 and later in this chapter as well, the contention of what makes a person a qualified agilist is still up in the air. Academia will need to understand and overcome this as they look to incorporate Agile to a greater degree.

Purpose to the People

As Agile continues to proliferate, enterprises will experience a dynamic shift within. Recruiting techniques, outsourcing practices, and management levels and styles will continue to evolve.

The role of the middle managers will continue to evolve

As discussed in Chapter 7, enterprises' shift toward working in a decentralized, Agile manner has impacted the role of the middle manager. Traditional obligations – such as assigning tasks, planning projects, reviewing work products, documenting progress, and evaluating employees – are being transitioned to other responsibilities that Agile creates. There is no consensus yet on exactly what this new role should be. Some suggest repurposing them as Product Owners (POs) or Scrum Masters (SMs) as most have the requisite institutional knowledge to succeed in that role; others, however, feel that this may lead to reporting conflicts, as team members don't feel they can be as open about failure and work in general. As Agile continues to evolve, the community will align on what this new role should be, standardizing until it becomes business as usual.

> "To remedy the challenges middle managers have, we need to support them on this shift in consciousness and mindset so they can in turn support the emergence and evolution of a more effective culture."
>
> **Michael K Sahota**, *SHIFT314*

Regardless of what this role looks like, most agree that the rest of the enterprise will need to bring significant resources to aid in this transition. Michael Sahota, speaker, trainer, and consultant at SHIFT314, further underscores the importance of this sentiment: "To remedy the challenges middle managers have, we need to support them on this shift in consciousness and mindset so they can in turn support the emergence and evolution of a more effective culture." With the support of those around them, middle managers and their role can fully evolve, decreasing the number of traditional managers, flattening the organization, and driving increased velocity and corporate agility.

Enterprises will rethink their co-location strategy

Historically, outsourcing has been an effective cost-saving measure for many corporations. This approach, however, has begun to lose its luster as international tariff wars and pandemics – like the coronavirus disease (COVID-19) pandemic – have many rethinking their supply chain strategies. Combined with the advent of Agile and its use cases, and a general shift in focus from ROI and labor arbitrage to flexible, adaptable, and innovative teams, outsourcing has further fallen out of favor, as shown in the graph on the next page. Looking into the future, as enterprises continually seek to improve communication, transparency, and collaboration, many will turn to co-location.

It is important to note, however, that this is not a quick fix for ineffective communication, as mistakenly used by some corporations. Colin Ferguson, Agile Transformation Principal at North Highland, underscores this sentiment: "The idea of having everybody co-located is ideal, but not always possible. What is equally and often more important is focusing on ways we can communicate more effectively regardless of physical proximity." The need for effective communication is further exemplified as, at times, unforeseen situations can force organizations, both large and small, to work from home, away from one another. Take, for example, the coronavirus disease (COVID-19) pandemic: most employees of organizations were forced to work from home. Those that implemented and practiced effective communication found success; others, did not. In the future, corporations will increasingly recognize that to sustain business continuity, but, more importantly, team effectiveness in general, co-location, for some, will be deprioritized in lieu of garnering truly effective communication.

> "The idea of having everybody co-located is ideal, but not always possible. What is equally and often more important is focusing on ways we can communicate more effectively regardless of physical proximity."
>
> **Colin Ferguson**, *North Highland*

Outsourcing Growth Trends

The growth of outsourcing in various industries has slowed.

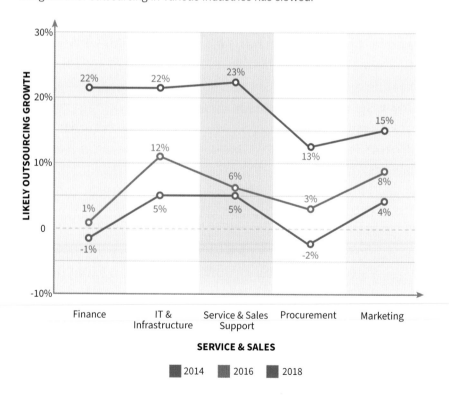

SERVICE & SALES

2014   2016   2018

Source: Adapted from Phil Fersht, 2018'

Generational values will align with an Agile culture

As discussed in Chapter 1, the workforce will evolve due in part to the preferences and values of today's younger generation. Although they represent a relatively small portion of the pie today, that portion will continue to grow until the aspects of an enterprise they value – the ability to share with each other, communicate through social platforms, and learn about what interests them – become the workplace norm.[8] This is advantageous to those utilizing Agile; not surprisingly, an Agile culture provides the flexibility and adaptability to support these changing values. Remember, however, these values will at some point also be subsumed by those of future generations. Agile, again, will enable corporations to adapt.

For example, Agile's focus on transparency will enable team members to share ideas and work openly with one another. Its prioritization of autonomy and self-governance allows team members to communicate in whatever platforms they find most efficient. Focus on cross-functionality empowers team members to learn different things, not just what they're good at. As you would guess, Agile and an Agile culture will find much success in the eyes of the up-and-coming workforce. And you wouldn't be alone in thinking this; many have gone so far as to design office spaces that would further augment the synergistic values of Agile and Millennials in the workplace.[9]

> "Agile enables the aspects of motivation that have always been relevant in the workplace: purpose, autonomy, mastery. It just happens to be that our workforce today is more receptive to it."
>
> **Max Ekesi**, *Whole Foods Market*

This is not to say, however, that Agile was forward-thinking and preemptively solved for the next generation's values; rather, Agile, as alluded to throughout the book, provides the tools to solve needs that are timeless – Millennials and beyond have just been more vocal about expressing them. Max Ekesi, Agile Program Manager at Whole Foods Market, shares the same sentiment: "Agile enables the aspects of motivation that have always been relevant in the workplace: purpose, autonomy, mastery. It just happens to be that our workforce today is more receptive to it."

Continuous Evolution

As Agile penetrates new markets, industries, and verticals, it will garner more and more feedback. As such, it will continue to iterate and adapt as necessitated by the marketplace.

The Agile certification bar will rise

In recent years, the Agile certification market has become flooded, both in the amount of certifications offered and the number of those desiring them. As the demand for practitioners in the enterprise has skyrocketed, so has the number of those qualifying themselves through a weekend "Certified ScrumMaster" course. Because of the ease of obtaining an Agile certification and the misaligned amount of perceived value it brings, there is often a mismatch between those whom corporations seek and the capability of those they actually hire.

> "Certifications are a decent start, and they're an indicator. But they certainly shouldn't be a hiring decision, the way they are now."
>
> **Scott Ambler,** *Disciplined Agile*

Through the guidance of the community and several Agile thought leaders like Scott Ambler, co-founder of Disciplined Agile, organizations have begun to understand the severity of this misalignment, prioritizing real experience in lieu of a piece of paper: "Certifications are a decent start, and they're an indicator. But they certainly shouldn't be a hiring decision, the way they are now."

This trend will continue into the future as current certifications fall out of favor for more strenuous ones. This has already begun to take place, with the Project Management Institute's Agile Certified Practitioner (ACP) program instituting arduous experience requirements: individuals need over 1500 hours of Agile experience to be eligible.

Emerging technology capabilities will augment Agile at scale

As Agile scales globally, enterprises will continue to pursue the best technologies to augment team communication and interactions. For example, the current landscape of tools includes the likes of Jira, Slack, Trello, and Asana, among many others. These tools do fine with regard to communicating with each other, but have a tough time incorporating customer feedback. As we look into the future, the evolution of these tools will enable streamlined interactions between your team members and with your customers as well. Anthony Olsen, Product Owner at Windstream Enterprise, feels the same: "They're all great in regards to what they are now; but, they lack the tie in from customers' feedback. In the future, we'll start seeing a lot more investment in the growth of these tools from a product ownership perspective."

> "They're all great in regards to what they are now; but, they lack the tie in from customers' feedback. In the future, we'll start seeing a lot more investment in the growth of these tools from a product ownership perspective."
>
> **Anthony Olsen**, *Windstream Enterprise*

Furthermore, as discussed in Chapter 1, the advent of emerging technologies will disrupt and evolve the workplace, and also augment

Spotlight

The Boundless Future of Agile

Art Moore
Clear Systems LLC, President

Through his time leading both government and commercial transformations and as Founder of Clear Systems LLC working with myriad teams and individuals, Art Moore has experienced firsthand the power of Agile values and principles to motivate people at all levels of an organization. He believes that Agile inspires people to believe in themselves and in others, and encourages them to form partnerships in the journey to corporate agility. It has also demonstrated to him that while frameworks and practices continue to mature in effectiveness, it is the awareness, collaboration, and action stimulated by the underlying values and principles of Agile that drive organizational change and sustainable improvements in business agility.

Moore goes on to say that most organizations, industries, and countries have only begun to tap into the potential benefits of Agile product delivery. New methods and technology – AI and DevOps – made it possible to get much closer to and deliver on customer needs, frequently and in new ways. Beyond that, Agile in conjunction with other transformation methodologies is causing us to broaden our definition of done and our view of success to include sustainable value to the client, ourselves, and society.

Moore adds that he believes the future possibilities of Agile are boundless. He encourages organizations to look to current leaders such as Netflix, Google, AWS and others to see what the future of Agile may hold. He goes on to quote Mik Kersten by saying, "Those who master large-scale software delivery will define the economic landscape of the 20th century."

The best way to future-proof yourself, Moore concludes, is not to rest on current practice but become lifelong learners. Identify resources to help you on your path to corporate agility, and use the values and principles of Agile to help guide you on your journey.

Agile at scale. Take, for example, the use of blockchain technology within an Agile environment. Many find that the two are highly synergistic, as they prioritize similar points: transparency, community, and self-organization.[10] Furthermore, many use cases have already been ideated and implemented. The popular study by Valentina Lenarduzzi and three other scholars, for example, explored an approach in which smart contracts are used to leverage part of the Product Owner duties.[11]

Looking to the Future

Thank you for reading the entirety of this book. There was a lot of information to digest, but in doing so, you are better prepared to not only more effectively engage Agile within your enterprise now, but in the future as well. Remember, Agile and its values and principles, its truths, do not solve for challenges or disruptions that are happening unique to now; rather, they solve for those that are timeless. The disruption that Walt Disney faced a hundred years ago is not so different from the disruption you face now or the disruption you'll face in the future. And, although how it manifests through technology, competitors, and customers may change, the characteristics necessary to circumvent them do not. Understand that, through Agile or otherwise, the need for corporate agility will never be subsumed.

This is not to say, however, that Agile itself won't change. Sutherland, van Bennekum, Cockburn, Kern, and the rest of the signatories knew this, that although Agile solves for the timeless fundamental challenges, it can always be more proficient and efficient in doing so. They knew that, by baking an iterative and adaptable approach into Agile, it would rise and proliferate. This is the true reason why Agile is so potent and why it will stand the test of time.

At the end of the day, you're living in today's world and the need to adapt and evolve is increasing and will only continue to do so. Stakes are high and the time to act is now, so share your newfound knowledge with your colleagues, teams, and corporation. All the best to you on your path to Corporate Agility, *huaka'i maika'i!*

ENDNOTES

Introduction

1. Matarelli, Maria. "This Is Why Fortune 500 Companies Use An Agile Approach To Process Improvement." Medium. ART marketing, November 21, 2017. https://artplusmarketing.com/this-is-why-fortune-500-companies-use-an-agile-approach-to-process-improvement-d4095d410a61.

2. Ajmal, Sajid. "How Agile Scrum Training Transformed These 5 Companies." QuickStart Technology Training. QuickStart, May 4, 2018. https://www.quickstart.com/blog/how-agile-scrum-training-transformed-these-5-companies.

3. "Agile Acquisition & Contracting in Government – 2017." REI Systems. Accessed April 30, 2020. https://www.reisystems.com/agile-acquisition-and-contracting-in-government-2017/.

4. "Survey Data Shows That Many Companies Are Still Not Truly Agile – Sponsor Content from CA Technologies." *Harvard Business Review*, March 29, 2018. https://hbr.org/sponsored/2018/03/survey-data-shows-that-many-companies-are-still-not-truly-agile.

Chapter 1

1. Chris, Joseph. "4 Walt Disney Leadership Style Principles." Joseph Chris Partners, August 15, 2015. http://www.josephchris.com/4-walt-disney-leadership-style-principles.

2. Pak, Eudie. "Walt Disney's Rocky Road to Success." Biography.com. A&E Networks Television, June 27, 2019. https://www.biography.com/news/walt-disney-failures.

3. Ibid.

4. Ibid.

5. Ibid.

6. Kim, Larry. "31 Surprising Facts About Walt Disney." Inc.com. Inc., April 29, 2015. https://www.inc.com/larry-kim/31-surprising-facts-about-walt-disney.html.

7. "Walter Elias Disney." *Entrepreneur*. Accessed January 5, 2020. https://www.entrepreneur.com/article/197528.

8. "Corporate Longevity: Turbulence Ahead for Large Organizations." Innosight, August 2016. https://www.innosight.com/wp-content/uploads/2016/08/Corporate-Longevity-2016-Final.pdf.

9. PricewaterhouseCoopers. "The Disruptors: How Five Key Factors Can Make or Break Your Business." PwC. Accessed April 30, 2020. https://www.pwc.com/gx/en/ceo-agenda/pulse/the-disruptors.html.

10. "Age and Tenure in the C-Suite: Korn Ferry Study Reveals Trends by Title and Industry." Korn Ferry, February 13, 2017. https://www.kornferry.com/about-us/press/age-and-tenure-in-the-c-suite-korn-ferry-institute-study-reveals-trends-by-title-and-industry.
"Age and tenure in the C-Suite: Korn Ferry Study Reveals Trends by Title and Industry." Korn Ferry, January 21, 2020. https://ir.kornferry.com/news-releases/news-release-details/age-and-tenure-c-suite-korn-ferry-study-reveals-trends-title-and.

11. Larcker, David and Brian Tayan. "CEO Compensation: Data." Stanford Graduate School of Business, January, 2019. https://www.gsb.stanford.edu/faculty-research/publications/ceo-compensation-data.

12. PricewaterhouseCoopers. "The Disruptors: How Five Key Factors Can Make or Break Your Business." PwC. Accessed April 30, 2020. https://www.pwc.com/gx/en/ceo-agenda/pulse/the-disruptors.html.

13. *Advertising, Week*. "How Netflix Uses Analytics to Thrive." HuffPost, December 8, 2017. https://www.huffpost.com/entry/how-netflix-uses-analytics-to-thrive_b_5a297879e4b053b5525db82b.

14. Carantit, Laurie. "Six Ways Big Data Has Changed the Workforce." International Association for Human Resources Information Management, June 21, 2018. https://ihrim.org/2018/06/six-ways-big-data-has-changed-the-workforce/.

15. Enthoven, Dan. "How Big Data Will Reinvent Performance Management." Inc.com. Inc., June 26, 2014. https://www.inc.com/daniel-enthoven/how-big-data-will-reinvent-performance-management.html.

16. Ibid.

17. "Walmart Case Study." Hyperledger. Accessed April 30, 2020. https://www.hyperledger.org/resources/publications/walmart-case-study.

18. Kessler, Sarah. "Robots Are Replacing Managers, Too." Quartz, July 31, 2017. https://qz.com/1039981/robots-are-replacing-managers-too/.

19. Chowdhry, Amit. "Artificial Intelligence to Create 58 Million New Jobs by 2022, Says Report." Forbes. *Forbes* magazine, September 18, 2018. https://www.forbes.com/sites/amitchowdhry/2018/09/18/artificial-intelligence-to-create-58-million-new-jobs-by-2022-says-report/#5a0472b54d4b.
"The Workforce of the Future: How Will Technology Impact the Manufacturing Industry?" Valamis, March 26, 2018. https://www.valamis.com/blog/the-workforce-of-the-future-how-will-technology-impact-the-manufacturing-industry.
Greenfield, David. "Planning for the Impact of Automation on Jobs." *Automation World*, January 31, 2019. https://www.automationworld.com/home/blog/13319522/planning-for-the-impact-of-automation-on-jobs.

20. "Global Organizations Face Significant Gaps in Enterprise Risk Management, According to New Riskonnect and Compliance Week Report." Business Wire, August 27, 2019. https://www.businesswire.com/news/home/20190827005132/en/Global-Organizations-Face-Significant-Gaps-Enterprise-Risk.

21. "Common Gaps in Enterprise Business Continuity Plans: Agility Recovery Blog." Agility Recovery, January 6, 2020. https://www.agilityrecovery.com/common-gaps-in-enterprise-business-continuity-plans/.

22. Doyle, Alison. "How Often Do People Change Jobs?" The Balance Careers, January 20, 2020. www.thebalancecareers.com/how-often-do-people-change-jobs-2060467.

23. Wolff, Allie. "The Top 5 Things Millennials Want in the Workplace." Hatchbuck. Accessed February 16, 2020. https://www.hatchbuck.com/blog/top-5-things-millennials-want-workplace/.

24. Ibid.

25. Brundage, Jeff. "What Is Organizational Transformation and When Is It Necessary?" OrgInc, April 18, 2019. https://www.orginc.com/blog/what-is-organizational-transformation-and-when-is-it-necessary.

26. Randolph, Marc. "Inside Netflix's Crazy, Doomed Sales Pitch to Blockbuster." Vanity Fair. Accessed April 30, 2020. https://www.vanityfair.com/news/2019/09/netflixs-crazy-doomed-meeting-with-blockbuster.

27. Poggi, Jeanine. "Blockbuster's Rise and Fall: The Long, Rewinding Road." TheStreet, September 23, 2010. https://www.thestreet.com/investing/stocks/the-rise-and-fall-of-blockbuster-the-long-rewinding-road-10867574.
Ben Unglesbee, "A Timeline of Blockbuster's Ride from Megahit to Flop." Retail Dive, October 7, 2019. https://www.retaildive.com/news/a-timeline-of-blockbusters-ride-from-megahit-to-flop/564305/.
"History of Netflix in Short." Brand Riddle. Accessed February 17, 2020. https://brandriddle.com/netflix-history/.
Casadesus-Masanell, Ramon, and Karen Elterman. "How Did Netflix Crush Blockbuster? The Importance of Business Model Interaction." Steemit, July 18, 2019. https://steemit.com/business/@casadesus/how-did-netflix-crush-blockbuster-the-importance-of-business-model-interaction.

28. "BlackBerry Turns 35: A Look Back at Its Big Transformation." BNN Bloomberg, March 7, 2019. https://www.bnnbloomberg.ca/blackberry-turns-35-a-look-back-at-its-big-transformation-1.1225242.

29. Jacobsen, Darcy. "5 Companies Whose Great Cultures Saved Their Bacon." Workhuman, April 8, 2014. https://www.workhuman.com/resources/globoforce-blog/5-companies-whose-great-cultures-saved-their-bacon.

30. Ibid.

31. Ibid.

Chapter 2

1. Varhol, Peter. "The Complete History of Agile Software Development." TechBeacon, January 22, 2019. https://techbeacon.com/app-dev-testing/agility-beyond-history-legacy-agile-development.

2. Ibid.

3. Sutherland, Jeff. Challenges of Agile and Advice to CEOs with Jeff Sutherland, Scrum Inc. YouTube, Scrum Alliance, October 25, 2018. https://www.youtube.com/watch?v=qaFSTSW_6Uo.

4. "5 Success Stories That Will Make You Believe in Scaled Agile." ObjectStyle. Accessed April 30, 2020. https://www.objectstyle.com/agile/scaled-agile-success-story-lessons.

5. Linders, Ben. "Benefits of Agile Transformation at Barclays." Disciplined Agile Consortium, September 8, 2016. https://disciplinedagileconsortium.org/resources/Pictures/Case%20studies/Benefits%20of%20Agile%20Transformation%20at%20Barclays.pdf.

6. Westland, Jason. "Understanding Scrum Methodology: A Guide." ProjectManager.com, January 11, 2018. https://www.projectmanager.com/blog/scrum-methodology.
"Exploring Key Elements of Spotify's Agile Scaling Model." Scaled Agile Tool for Distributed PI Planning. Kendis, July 23, 2018. https://kendis.io/spotify/exploring-key-elements-spotifys-agile-scaling-model/.
"What Is Continuous Integration?" Agile Alliance, September 24, 2019. https://www.agilealliance.org/glossary/continuous-integration/.
Meyer, Robinson. "The Secret Startup That Saved the Worst Website in America." *The Atlantic*. Atlantic Media Company, July 10, 2015. https://www.theatlantic.com/technology/archive/2015/07/the-secret-startup-saved-healthcare-gov-the-worst-website-in-america/397784/.

7. "Universal Credit: Early Progress – National Audit Office (NAO) Report." National Audit Office, September 5, 2013. https://www.nao.org.uk/report/universal-credit-early-progress-2/.

8. Murphy, Margi. "Agile Project Failure Kills £15m Surrey Police System." *Computerworld*, June 20, 2014. https://www.computerworld.com/article/3418153/agile-project-failure-kills--15m-surrey-police-system.html.

9. Mersino, Anthony. "Agile Transformations Take Too Long - A Cautionary Tale." Vitality Chicago Inc., August 31, 2018. https://vitalitychicago.com/blog/agile-transformations-take-too-long-a-cautionary-tale/.

Chapter 3

1. Prosci. "Stop Confusing Agile with Agile." Prosci. Accessed January 20, 2020. https://www.prosci.com/resources/articles/stop-confusing-agile-with-agile.

2. "Manifesto for Agile Software Development." Manifesto for Agile Software Development, February 13, 2001. http://agilemanifesto.org/.

3. Ibid.

4. Tabbaa, Bishr. "Small Is Beautiful – The Big Bang Launch Failure of Healthcare.gov." Coiner Blog, October 29, 2018. https://coinerblog.com/small-is-beautiful-the-launch-failure-of-healthcare-gov-5e60f20eb967/.

5. "The Failed Launch of www.HealthCare.gov." Technology and Operations Management, November 18, 2016. https://digital.hbs.edu/platform-rctom/submission/the-failed-launch-of-www-healthcare-gov/.

6. Ibid.

7. Tabbaa, Bishr. "Small Is Beautiful -The Big Bang Launch Failure of Healthcare.gov." Coiner Blog, October 29, 2018. https://coinerblog.com/small-is-beautiful-the-launch-failure-of-healthcare-gov-5e60f20eb967/.

8. "Where Did HealthCare.gov Go Wrong? Let's Start with 'Everywhere.'" SmartBear.com, April 3, 2014. https://smartbear.com/blog/collaborate/where-did-healthcare-gov-go-wrong-lets-start-with/.

9. Sutherland, Jeff. "The Scrum@Scale Guide - A Definitive Guide to the Scrum@Scale Framework." Scrum@Scale, March 2020. https://www.scrumatscale.com/scrum-at-scale-guide-read-online/.

10. Sutherland, Jeff. "The Scrum@Scale Guide." Scrum at Scale, March 15, 2020. http://www.scrumatscale.com/wp-content/uploads/ScrumatScaleGuide-Published3.15.20.DrJeffSutherland.pdf.

11. Ibid.

12. Sutherland, Jeff, J.J. Sutherland, *Scrum: The Art of Doing Twice the Work in Half the Time* (London: Random House Business, 2014).

13. "Joe Justice: How a $149B Company Sped Up 175% with Scrum at Scale." Scrum@Scale. Accessed January 18, 2020. https://www.scrumatscale.com/project/joe-justice-how-a-149b-company-sped-up-175-with-scrum-at-scale/.

14. "What Is Kanban? An Overview of the Kanban Method." Digite. Accessed March 21, 2020. https://www.digite.com/kanban/what-is-kanban/.

15. Ibid.

16. "What Is Agile Kanban Methodology?" Inflectra. Accessed May 1, 2020. https://www.inflectra.com/methodologies/kanban.aspx.

17. "What Is the Kanban Method?" Kanban University. Accessed March 10, 2020. https://www.kanban.university/.

18. "GE Aviation Czech Case Study: Lean Team Boosted Its Productivity during New Aircraft Engine Program." Kanbanize. Accessed May 1, 2020. https://kanbanize.com/kanban-resources/case-studies/kanban-aerospace-case-study.

19. Ambler, Scott, and Mark Lines. "Intro to Disciplined Agile: Disciplined Agile." Disciplined Agile Consortium. Accessed March 16, 2020. https://www.pmi.org/disciplined-agile/introduction-to-disciplined-agile.

20. Ambler, Scott, and Mark Lines. "Risk Value Lifecycle – Disciplined Agile (DA)." Disciplined Agile Consortium. Accessed May 1, 2020. https://www.pmi.org/disciplined-agile/lifecycle/risk-value-lifecycle#Lifecycle.

21. Ambler, Scott, and Mark Lines. "Transforming from Traditional to Disciplined Agile Delivery." Disciplined Agile Consortium. Accessed May 9, 2020. https://disciplinedagileconsortium.org/resources/Pictures/Case%20studies/Panera%20Case%20Study.pdf.

22. Linders, Ben. "Benefits of Agile Transformation at Barclays." InfoQ, September 8, 2016. https://www.infoq.com/news/2016/09/benefits-agile-barclays/.

23. "What Is SAFe | Scaled Agile." Scale Agile Framework. Accessed March 16, 2020. https://www.scaledagile.com/enterprise-solutions/what-is-safe/.

24. "Case Study – Cisco." Scaled Agile Framework. Accessed January 5, 2020. https://www.scaledagileframework.com/cisco-case-study/.

25. "Case Study – Air France – KLM." Scaled Agile Framework. Accessed January 5, 2020. https://www.scaledagileframework.com/case-study-air-france-klm/.

26. "CollabNet VersionOne Releases 13th Annual State of Agile Report." CollabNet VersionOne, May 7, 2019. https://www.collab.net/news/press/collabnet-versionone-releases-13th-annual-state-agile-report.

27. Salameh, Abdallah, and Julian M. Bass. "Spotify Tailoring for Promoting Effectiveness in Cross-Functional Autonomous Squads." SpringerLink. Springer, Cham, August 31, 2019. https://link.springer.com/chapter/10.1007/978-3-030-30126-2_3.

28. "Company Info." Spotify. Accessed May 1, 2020. https://newsroom.spotify.com/company-info/.

29. Ibid.

30. Denning, Steve. "Can Big Organizations Be Agile?" *Forbes* magazine, November 26, 2016. https://www.forbes.com/sites/stevedenning/2016/11/26/can-big-organizations-be-agile/#e41f30538e79.

Chapter 5

1. Sutherland, Jeff. Challenges of Agile and Advice to CEOs with Jeff Sutherland, Scrum Inc. YouTube, Scrum Alliance, October 25, 2018. https://www.youtube.com/watch?v=qaFSTSW_6Uo.

2. Rudenko, Olga. "Guide to Agile Transformation: Plans, Challenges and Case Studies: Expert360." Expert 360, November 17, 2017. https://expert360.com/resources/articles/agile-transformation-strategy-plan.

3. Wofford, Chris. "Empower Your Team Through Servant Leadership." #Cornell360, September 9, 2018. https://blog.ecornell.com/empower-your-team-through-servant-leadership/.

4. Wilkinson, David. "Is the Change Curve a Myth?" *The Oxford Review*, March 3, 2016. https://www.oxford-review.com/is-the-change-curve-real/.

5. Joseph, Tanisha. "Organizational Transformational Frameworks: Big Bang & Phased Frameworks." KnowledgeHut Blog, August 17, 2018. https://www.knowledgehut.com/blog/project-management/big-bang-and-phased-approaches-how-to-do-it-and-what-to-expect.

Chapter 6

1. "Summary of Rogers' Adoption Curve." Value Based Management. Accessed March 12, 2020. https://www.valuebasedmanagement.net/methods_rogers_innovation_adoption_curve.html.

2. Ibid.

3. Fuda, Peter. "15 Qualities of a Transformational Change Agent." Charter for Compassion. Accessed May 1, 2020. https://charterforcompassion.org/leadership-and-business/15-qualities-of-a-transformational-change-agent.

4. "Communication on Agile Software Teams." Communication on Agile Software Teams. Accessed May 1, 2020. http://www.agilemodeling.com/essays/communication.htm.

5. Pressman, Matt. "Elon Musk: You Should Be Failing. 'If Things Are Not Failing, You Are Not Innovating Enough." CleanTechnica, February 1, 2020. https://cleantechnica.com/2020/02/01/elon-musk-you-should-be-failing-if-things-are-not-failing-you-are-not-innovating-enough/.

6. Ibid.

7. Shahan, Zachary. "Tesla Sales Grew 47× in 7 Years." CleanTechnica, January 3, 2020. https://cleantechnica.com/2020/01/03/tesla-sales-grew-47x-in-7-years/.
   Ferris, Robert. "Tesla Recalling 53,000 Vehicles Due to Faulty Parking Brake." NBCNews.com. NBCUniversal News Group, April 20, 2017. https://www.nbcnews.com/business/autos/tesla-recalling-53-000-vehicles-due-faulty-parking-brake-n748981.

8. Linders, Ben, David Spinks, and Glaudia Califano. "Agile around the World – A Journey of Discovery." InfoQ, August 24, 2019. https://www.infoq.com/articles/agile-around-world/.

9. Data from Erin Meyer, *Being the Boss in Brussels, Boston, and Beijing*. Accessed April 2, 2020.
   Data from Christopher Soh, *Brazil: A Cross-Cultural Perspective for Global Managers*. Accessed April 2, 2020.

Data from Sharon Glazer, *The Role of Culture in Decision Making*. Accessed April 2, 2020.

Data from Chris Carr, *Strategic Investment Decisions and Short-Termism: Germany Versus Britain*. Accessed April 2, 2020.

Data from Selcen Ozturkcan, *Management Practices in Kingdom of Saudi Arabia: Exploring Perspectives of Saudi Managers and Middle East Expats*. Accessed April 2, 2020.

Data from Claudio Cirocco, *Cultural Considerations When Doing Business in Argentina*. Accessed April 2, 2020.

Data from Hofstede Insights, *What about Argentina?* Accessed April 2, 2020.

Data from Hofstede Insights, *What about Kenya?* Accessed April 2, 2020.

Data from Charlotte Jonasson, *Rethinking the Harmonious Family: Processes of Social Organization in a Korean Corporation*. Accessed April 2, 2020.

Data from Balasubramaniam Ramesh, Lan Cao, Jongwoo Kim, Kannan Mohan, Tabitha L. James, *Consider Culture When Implementing Agile Practices*. Accessed April 2, 2020.

Data from Joakim Eriksson, *Analyzing Potential Barriers of Agile Adoption in Chinese Software Development Organizations*. Accessed April 2, 2020.

Data from Hajer Ayed, Benoit Vanderose, Naji Habra, *Agile Cultural Challenges in Europe and Asia: Insights from Practitioners*. Accessed April 2, 2020.

Data from Viva Sarah Press, *Taking Care of Business: Essential Tips on How Best to Work with Israelis*. Accessed April 2, 2020.

Data from Tech Heights, *What Characterizes Israeli Business Culture?* Accessed April 2, 2020.

Chapter 7

1. ScrumAlliance. Accessed April 2, 2020. https://www.scrumalliance.org/get-certified/scrum-master-track/certified-scrummaster.
   PMI. Accessed April 2, 2020. https://www.pmi.org/certifications/types/agile-acp?utm_job_number=11.
   Scaled Agile Framework. Accessed April 2, 2020. https://www.scaledagileframework.com/safe-program-consultant/.
   ICAgile. Accessed April 2, 2020. https://www.icagile.com/Agile-Delivery/Agile-Coaching/Agile-Coaching.
   ScrumAlliance. Accessed April 2, 2020. https://www.scrumalliance.org/get-certified/scrum-master-track/advanced-certified-scrummaster.

2. Cohn, Mike. "Four Types of Resistors When Adopting Agile." Mountain Goat Software, December 2, 2009. https://www.mountaingoatsoftware.com/blog/four-types-of-resistors-when-adopting-Agile.

3. Manzoni, Jean-François, and Jean-Louis Barsoux. "The Set-Up-to-Fail Syndrome." *Harvard Business Review*, March 1998. https://hbr.org/1998/03/the-set-up-to-fail-syndrome.

4. Markey, Rob, and Fred Reichheld. "Introducing: The Net Promoter System®." Bain, December 8, 2011. https://www.bain.com/insights/introducing-the-net-promoter-system-loyalty-insights/.

5. De Smet, Aaron, Daidree Tofano, and Chris Smith. "How Companies Can Help Midlevel Managers Navigate Agile Transformations." McKinsey & Company, April 10, 2019. https://www.mckinsey.com/business-functions/organization/our-insights/how-companies-can-help-midlevel-managers-navigate-Agile-transformations.

6. Ibid.

7. Hayes, Adam. "Peter Principle: What You Need to Know." Investopedia, June 25, 2019. https://www.investopedia.com/terms/p/peter-principle.asp.

Chapter 8

1. "Core Practices for Agile/Lean Documentation." Agile Modeling. Accessed May 1, 2020. http://www.agilemodeling.com/essays/agileDocumentationBestPractices.htm#JustSimpleEnough.

2. Sutherland, Jeff. "Challenges of Agile and Advice to CEOs with Jeff Sutherland, Scrum Inc." YouTube, Scrum Alliance, October 25, 2018. https://www.youtube.com/watch?v=qaFSTSW_6Uo.

Chapter 9

1. Bean, Randy, and Thomas H. Davenport. "Companies Are Failing in Their Efforts to Become Data-Driven." *Harvard Business Review*, February 5, 2019. https://hbr.org/2019/02/companies-are-failing-in-their-efforts-to-become-data-driven.

2. Bean, Randy. "Big Data and AI Executive Survey." Boston, MA: NewVantage Partners LLC, January, 2020. http://newvantage.com/wp-content/uploads/2020/01/NewVantage-Partners-Big-Data-and-AI-Executive-Survey-2020-1.pdf.

3. Paine, Katie. "Evaluating Your CSR? Here Are Activity Measures and Outcome Metrics You Need to Use." *The Measurement Advisor*, May 11, 2018. http://painepublishing.com/measurementadvisor/evaluating-your-csr-here-are-activity-measures-and-outcome-metrics-you-need-to-use/.

4. "OKRs." Medium, November 28, 2014. https://medium.com/startup-tools/okrs-5afdc298bc28.

5. "How Netflix Nearly Lost Its Footing and What It Did to Recover." Teampay, February 19, 2019. https://www.teampay.co/insights/netflix-recession/.

6. Ibid.

Chapter 10

1. Markey, Rob, and Fred Reichheld. "Introducing: The Net Promoter System®." Bain, December 8, 2011. https://www.bain.com/insights/introducing-the-net-promoter-system-loyalty-insights/.

2. "Net Promoter®." Bain. Accessed May 1, 2020. https://www.netpromotersystem.com/about/.

3. "What Is a Good Net Promoter Score? (2020 NPS Benchmark)." Retently, March 6, 2020. https://www.retently.com/blog/good-net-promoter-score/.

4. Hammer, Michael. "Reengineering Work: Don't Automate, Obliterate." *Harvard Business Review*. Accessed January 5, 2020. https://hbr.org/1990/07/reengineering-work-dont-automate-obliterate.

5. "Business Process Reengineering: History, Application, and Method." Overhead Watch, December 29, 2016. https://overheadwatch.com/business-process-reengineering/.

6. Pearson, Sonia. "Business Process Reengineering (BPR): Definition, Steps, Examples." Tallyfy, February 26, 2020. https://tallyfy.com/business-process-reengineering/#Business_Process_Reengineering_Steps.

7. McCormick, Michael. "Waterfall vs. Agile Methodology." August 9, 2012. http://mccormickpcs.com/images/Waterfall_vs_Agile_Methodology.pdf.

8. "SDLC – Overview." Tutorialspoint. Accessed May 1, 2020. https://www.tutorialspoint.com/sdlc/sdlc_overview.htm.

9. Dam, Rikke Friis, and Yu Siang Teo. "Design Thinking: Get a Quick Overview of the History." The Interaction Design Foundation. Accessed May 1, 2020. https://www.interaction-design.org/literature/article/design-thinking-get-a-quick-overview-of-the-history.

10. "What Is Design Thinking?" The Interaction Design Foundation. Accessed May 1, 2020. https://www.interaction-design.org/literature/topics/design-thinking.

11. Subiksha, Miriam. "Design Thinking and Agile Methodology for Innovation – DZone Agile." dzone.com. DZone, November 28, 2018. https://dzone.com/articles/design-thinking-and-agile-methodology-for-innovati.

12. "Agile and Design Thinking at IBM." LinkedIn SlideShare, June 17, 2017. https://www.slideshare.net/uxpin/agile-and-design-thinking-at-ibm.

13. "Six Experts' Definitions – What Is Six Sigma?" Vetter Blog. Accessed January 5, 2020. https://www.getvetter.com/posts/195-six-experts-definitions-what-is-six-sigma.

14. Kumar, Pankaj. "What Is Six Sigma: A Complete Overview." Simplilearn, April 13, 2020. https://www.simplilearn.com/what-is-six-sigma-a-complete-overview-article.

15. "What Is Six Sigma?" *Six Sigma Daily*, January 9, 2020. https://www.sixsigmadaily.com/what-is-six-sigma/.

16. Reidenbach, R. Eric. "Resurgence of Six Sigma in the Call Center: Decreasing Customer Churn." Process Excellence Network, Feburary 8, 2010. https://www.processexcellencenetwork.com/lean-six-sigma-business-performance/articles/resurgence-of-six-sigma-in-the-call-center-decreas.

17. Millard, Maggie. "The Fundamentals of the Lean Methodology." Kainexus, August 29, 2018. https://blog.kainexus.com/the-fundamentals-of-the-lean-methodology.

18. Ibid.

19. "DevOps: Principles, Practices, and DevOps Engineer Role." AltexSoft. August 30, 2018. https://www.altexsoft.com/blog/engineering/devops-principles-practices-and-devops-engineer-role/.

20. "6 Principles of DevOps." DevOps Agile Skills Association (DASA). Accessed May 1, 2020. https://www.devopsagileskills.org/dasa-devops-principles/.

21. Ibid.

Chapter 11

1. Arnold, Travis. "Roundup: Agile Marketing Manifestos," May 16, 2012. https://travisarnold.com/agile-marketing-manifestos/.

2. Schindler, Seth, and Juan Miguel Kanai. "How Mega Infrastructure Projects in Africa, Asia and Latin America Are Reshaping Development." The Conversation, October 31, 2019. https://theconversation.com/how-mega-infrastructure-projects-in-africa-asia-and-latin-america-are-reshaping-development-125449.

3. Jonnalagadda, Kalyan, Dave Fleisch, Pete Hultman, and Steve Berez. "How Agile Is Powering Healthcare Innovation." Bain, June 20, 2019. https://www.bain.com/insights/how-agile-is-powering-healthcare-innovation/.

4. Ibid.

5. Ali, Javaid. "Teaching Agile at Universities." Agile ME, April 15, 2015. https://www.slideshare.net/AgileME/teaching-agile-at-universities-by-javaid-ali.

6. Ibid.

7. Fersht, Phil. "Offshore Outsourcing Died with Trump. Now Value-Based Partnerships Are Rising from the Ashes..." Horses for Sources, April 28, 2018. https://www.horsesforsources.com/offshoring-IT-trump_042918.

8. "The Agile Generational Workforce." Cprime Training Center, March 11, 2014. https://www.slideshare.net/cPrime/agile-generational-workforce.

9. "Design an Agile Office for 2020." Ukhuni. Accessed January 30, 2020. https://www.ukhuni.co.za/blog/design-an-agile-office-for-2020/.

10. Jiang, Bob. "Blockchain and Agile." Medium, June 19, 2018. https://medium.com/bitfwd/blockchain-and-agile-cd3920d7c815.

11. Lenarduzzi, Valentina. "Blockchain Applications for Agile Methodologies." Research Gate, May 2018. https://www.researchgate.net/publication/325644177_Blockchain_applications_for_Agile_methodologies.

GLOSSARY

Agile: A way of working, also known as capital-A Agile or doing Agile, that adheres to Agile ceremonies, tools, roles, and structures.

agile: A way of thinking, also known as lowercase-a agile or being agile, that focuses on understanding and internalizing the Agile values and principles.

Agile Manifesto: A set of four values and twelve principles developed by software development visionaries in 2001 that addresses frustrations with traditional process shortfalls and issues by delivering interactively and continuously.

Agile Release Train (ART): A seasoned group of Agile teams that incrementally develops, delivers, and, where applicable, operates one or more solutions in an enterprise's value stream.

Agilessons: Pragmatic Agile transformation insights on how to realize corporate agility and rapidly evolve in the face of accelerating disruption from industry leaders who have lived and thrived through Agile transformations.

Blockchain: A continuously growing list of records called blocks, secured using cryptography, with every transaction being added chronologically, making a chain, and usually maintained across several computers that are linked in a peer-to-peer network.

Business Process Reengineering (BPR): A transformation methodology that focuses on fundamentally restructuring business processes from the ground-up to more efficiently drive business outcomes.

Co-location: A common Agile practice that moves core team members to the same physical space to maximize a team's coordination, problem solving, communication, and learning.

DayBlink: An award-winning, minority-owned, management consulting firm behind *Corporate Agility* and the Agilessons that provides deep expertise in strategic, technical, and transformational programs to United States and International clients.

Design Thinking: A different approach to product design and development that reframes user problems in a human-centric way to advance innovative solutions.

Detractor: An individual involved or impacted by an Agile transformation who is unhappy or finds fault with the company, its brand, and/or its products and/or services.

DevOps: A professional and cultural relationship practice between software development and IT operations, which extends Agile principles from software design through production deployment and operations.

Disciplined Agile (DA): Initially developed by Agile visionaries Scott Ambler and Mark Lines, DA is a people-first, learning-oriented hybrid Agile approach to IT solution delivery that has a risk-value delivery life cycle.

Extreme Programming (XP): An Agile software development methodology advocating short development cycles and frequent releases, which emphasizes teamwork. XP is designed to improve the overall quality of software by successfully adapting to the evolving needs of customers.

Fake Agile: Also known as Dark Agile and characterized as practicing Agile structures and processes – doing Agile – without embodying the values and principles of Agile – being agile.

Healthcare.gov: A health insurance exchange website often considered as the most infamous Agile failure; in its first week of launch, only 1% of users were able to use the site properly.

Kanban: A workflow management method that breaks project activities into small delivery increments. These increments are tracked on a physical or virtual board, providing transparency to the team and stakeholders. It is derived from a Japanese word that translates to "visual signal" or "card."

Key Performance Indicator (KPI): A measurable value that shows how effectively an enterprise is achieving a key business objective.

Large-Scale Scrum (LeSS): An Agile methodology developed by Bas Vodde and Craig Larman designed to apply the principles, purposes, and elements of Scrum in a large-scale context, but as simply as possible.

Lean: A way of working inspired by the management philosophy of Toyota Production Systems, which focuses on increasing customer value while minimizing risk and decreasing waste through continuous improvement.

Lean Six Sigma (LSS): A flexible and hybrid process improvement methodology that combines principles and aspects of Lean and Six Sigma to reduce cost and eliminate waste.

Media Richness Theory (MRT): A theory proposed by Richard Daft and Robert Lengel that is used to define the ability of different communications mediums to transfer information, with the highest being face-to-face communication and the lowest being emails and texts.

Minimum Viable Product (MVP): The simple version of the solution that can be tested by stakeholders and that allows for multiple incremental and continuous solution improvements.

Nail and Scale: An approach first popularized by Nathan R. Furr and Paul Ahlstrom in their book *Nail It Then Scale It*, which encourages enterprises to start small with a pilot group, then iteratively scale throughout the organization, learning from your successes and failures.

Net Promoter Score (NPS): A scaled scoring method created by Fred Reichheld that measures customer loyalty on a scale of –100 to 100, by asking customers one question: "On a scale from zero to ten, how likely are you to recommend this product or company to a friend or colleague?"

Retrospective: A Scrum ceremony held at the end of a Sprint iteration to support continuous improvement for the Scrum team, where it reviews its processes and ways of working with the spirit of celebrating successes and identifying improvement opportunities.

Scaled Agile Framework (SAFe): A framework created by Dean Leffingwell that applies Lean and Agile principles enterprise-wide using four levels: team, program, large solution, and portfolio.

Scrum: An Agile project management framework that includes a set of ceremonies with defined cadences, tools, and roles to help teams collaborate and self-organize to solve business problems.

Scrum@Scale: A modular approach to scaling Scrum by Dr. Jeff Sutherland and Alex Brown, which takes the basics of the Scrum framework and extends it to organizations and teams of all sizes, allowing companies to create their own Agile operating system.

Scrumban: A hybrid Agile development methodology that emerged to meet the needs of teams who want to minimize the batching of work and adopt a pull-based system, providing the structure of Scrum with the flexibility and visualization of Kanban.

Self-Organizing Team: A team that has the autonomy and authority to make decisions and choose how best to manage their own work, responsibilities, and timelines.

Servant Leadership: A leadership quality in which one prioritizes the needs of the group over his or her own. Embracing this style can often increase teamwork and build stronger relationships.

Six Sigma: A methodology popularized by General Electric in the 1980s. It utilizes six standard deviations as a benchmark to reduce variance and defects within a process.

Spotify Model: A unique approach to Agile used by Spotify Technology S.A. that organizes a network of Tribes, Squads, Chapters, and Guilds to scale efficiently across the corporation.

Sprint: An iteration cycle, usually one to four weeks in duration, used by Scrum teams to deliver small incremental solution components to provide business value to stakeholders.

Standup: A Scrum ceremony where teams regularly meet to share accomplishments, objectives, and impediments for the active Sprint.

Waterfall: A project management approach that segments project activities into serial stages where no stage can start prior to the completion of the previous one.

ACKNOWLEDGMENTS

Writing a book was harder than I thought and more rewarding than I could have ever imagined. The completion of this undertaking could not have been possible without the participation and assistance of so many people, and their contributions are sincerely appreciated and gratefully acknowledged.

This work has been developed through a series of interviews, calling on the experiences and insights of business leaders from various industries. We want to thank Arie van Bennekum, Marcus Johnson, Louis Toth, Phil Koserowski, Allen Broome, Vamsi Tirnati, Michael Piker, Steve Elliott, Max Ekesi, Kishore Koduri, Laurie Nicoletti, Sondra Ashmore, Gilli Aliotti, Anthony Olsen, Elaine Stone, Dr. Steve Mayner, Ashley Craft Fiore, Junius Rowland, Joshua Jones, Susan Marricone, Scott Ambler, Michael Sahota, Steven Ma, Jennifer Morelli, Linda Rising, Stacey Ackerman, Bob Payne, David Fisher, Dave Witkin, Art Moore, Crawfurd Hill, Colin Ferguson, Christen McLemore, and those of you who wished to remain unnamed for sharing your Agile journeys and for allowing us to disseminate your insights to the business world.

This book couldn't have been realized without the editorial and production efforts of Vicki Adang, Alexandra Battey, Zach Gajewski, Brian Neill, Wendy Palitz, Deborah Schindlar, Julie Trelstad, and Karen Weller.

And, to all my DayBlink colleagues, thank you for continuously pushing this project to do better and be better, and for helping to turn my vision into a reality. I genuinely appreciate the weekends, late nights, and hard work needed to make it all happen. Specifically, I would like to thank Wicar Akhtar, Shelby Balius, Preston Bradham, Gene Chen, Sharief Elgamal, Syed Hamzah, Chris Kokotilo, Daniel Kruse, Brian Morrison, Joseph Murray, Nick Novarro, Danielle Rosenfeld, Kim Shill, Nick Suarez, Jonathan Wilmot, Samuel Yanez, and Christa Zubic for the enhanced contributions on this project.

INDEX